OUTSOURCING BRINGS WHAT BENEFITS

TO ORGANIZATIONS

JOHN LOK

Contents

This book explains how and why outsource strategy, it can help educational and business aspects development. This book divides two parts. The first part explains why US outsourcing strategy can influence global wealth inequality to influence economy. Then, the second part explains why outsouring educational strategy can influence the country's education development and explains why Asia countries schools will need more outsouring educational teachers to teach their domestic students to get more benefits to employ domestic teachers.

This book first part indicates outsourcing is popular strategy to any global organizations. But outsourcing strategy has also disadvantages to influence economy. It concerns to explain why outsourcing strategy can bring benefits to some organizations, but it can also bring disadvantages to some organizations. I shall indicate evidences to explain why some organizations choose outsourcing strategy is not right. Consequently, organizations need to analyze their situations whether are suitable to apply outsourcing strategy to operate their management, before they decide to make outsourcing strategy. The major aim is to explain why outsourcing is one main factor influence global wealth inequality to developing countries.

This book second part aims to explain why productivity and education has close relationship to influence developing Asia countries' economic growth nowadays. Moreover, I shall indicate how growth theory can support it has relationship between education and economic productivity. Also, I shall indicate how the two different channels through which human capital can affect long run economic growth by education provision to developing Asia countries.

I shall explain how measure of the relationship between outsourcing education and productivity and economic growth can be quantified clearing to developing Asia of developing countries. Next, I shall explain how to measure of the growth rate of productivity to the average level or growth rate of education within any developing Asia countries. Finally, I shall indicate how outsoucing education can affect economic growth in developing Asia countries for long term. This book is suitable to any economy students, teachers or any readers who enjoy to learn why outsoucing and educational strategies have close relationship.

PROLOGUE

Bibliography

Outsourcing strategy brings business benefits

I

Information Technology Outsourcing

In any organization information technology department, information system operations remain the predominant function outsourced, other functions are also being performed by external service providers and the relationship is between outsourcing and certain demographics: size, industry is formation intensity. The results suggest that system operations remain being performed by external service providers. Further, industry and information intensity has some influence on the extent of outsourcing of certain functions.

The first reason is cost reduction, trying to remain competitive and up-to-date is becoming a financial burden to many organizations. This is true particularly in fields, such as banking and financial services, health care and manufacturing. Hiring outsiders to handle part or even all of its information system often helps an organization to provide better services and maintain a competitive advantage. The information technology industry choice of outsourcing factor is related to size, industry type and information technology.

The second reason is technological and/or human resources in the management of the information technology infrastructure skill improvement. The information technology department outsourcing service to external service provider, includes the degree of internalization of technological resources and the degree of internalization of human resources. Some economists defined internalization of outsourcing service is as ownership is by the focal organization which takes on full control with profit and loss responsibility.

Also who define outsourcing is as involving a significant use of resources, either technological and/or human resources, external to the organizational hierarchy in the management of the information technology infrastructure. So the information technology external service providers includes: applications development and maintenance, systems operations, networks/telecommunications management and user computing support, system planning and management purchase of application software, but excludes business consulting services, after-sale vendor services and the lease of telephone lines etc. outsourcing services.

The third reason is economics of scale in areas of hardware, software. This pressure is seen as the most significant factor driving today's corporate interest. An outsourcing service provision might be in a position to exploit economics of scale in areas of hardware, software and staff since it pools different kind of technological projects from many service receivers.

Outsourcing information technological service can reduce the corporate's cost with the high level of IT investment, there are increasing pressures to move away from fixed expenditure, corporate overhead towards a more direct variable cost approach to control the IT operations. The IT costs can become predictable for overruns is often placed on the service provider. Outsourcing service can allow the service to gain immediate access to competitiveness in delivering products or services as well as to avoid of obsolescence risk, due to the changes in the nature of the IT infrastructure, the risk of obsolescence is high. Outsourcing can allow the service provider has the ability to diversify these risks across a broad range of service receivers. However, long term contracts might in spread the risk, the weakness is back to the receiver.

It seems outsourcing IT service has also these disadvantages: such as, loss of flexibility or managerial control. Outsourcing reduces real or perceived control over both quality real or perceived control over both the quality of software and the timetable of project since the work is now being carried out by people not under direct supervision. It also threats to long term career prospects to information system professionals because many of them do not find suitable. Is jobs or promising career paths in both areas of the corporation.

Outsourcing also increases coordination cost. It may requires increasing time to communicate and coordinate with the service provider. Traditionally, the formal meeting cost of negotiating and monitoring the outsourcing contract are potentially wide ranging, indirect and substantial increasing, such as, additional releasing or transferring employees, in license transfer by software vendors and in re-negotiating contracts costs. So, the IT industry of profit motivates service provider might not be in the least interests of the outsourcing service receivers. Some IT service providers are in the business of maximizing their profit at any cost, this could run counter to a service receiver's interest.

Outsourcing or insourcing in human resource supply chain factor

To choosing of outsourcing or insourcing in human resource supply chain factor of the controlling service demanders needs to concern this issues: Should human resource activities be provided in house or should all or past of those activities be outsourced? The relationship between organizational structure and the HR function is an important variable. The individual activities that comprise HR systems include not only the employee life cycle from recruiting to termination, but also planning for organizational staffing needs and improving organizational effectiveness. How organizations need to outsource HR function to not care employees knowledge and skill is a factor to influence any organizations choose to outsourcing non core employees when which have no any right employees to be promoted to do the position. For example, firms engage in HR outsourcing to reduce management access HR expertise, achieve workforce flexibility, focus managerial resources and keep up with changing workplace negotiations. Also, supporting the tend is the availability of common technology platform, which can reduce costs for organizations and risks. However, organizations are afraid of losing some control over delivery of outsourcing services and finding themselves dependent on the vendor or liable for the vendors actions where there are both benefits and challenges may be informed by the structure of the relationship between client firms and these organizations offering the outsourced activities to client firms.

What variables are impacted by HR outsourcing of staffing? Which include: administrative costs for labor expense, client firm to HR relations, HR regulatory competency requirement, knowledge of cost factors, e.g. billing and pay rates, vendor markups and margins, vendor management competency requirement, client and vendor relationship, communication is between client managers and staffing vendor, employee data-available, data quality control, data security, match with job requirement, employee quality, inter-vendor competition, mining of client talent by vendor , quality content for preferred staffing vendor, standardization of business process (intra-company), strategic focus of client firm, demands on client managers vendor competency and external economic environmental viability.

However, it has dynamic relationship between the client firms and staffing vendors. Moreover, the models of human resource supply chain, every has different set of advantages and disadvantages for the client firms. The models can be relate to the decision making process on outsourcing of human resources. As strategic services tactic decisions have an important impact or selecting the particular HR outsourcing model that a client firm adopter. The another model is the balance of power and control over managing the control workers differ to decide what every worker individual skills or abilities outsourcing demand. Moreover, local contracting is also the predominant traditional model for outsourcing staffing with non-core employees. A client firm usually uses several staffing vendors to meet temporary staffing needs for seasonal functions, employee absences and special projects. The advantages of local contracting are high touch and high quality of service by staffing vendors, minimal bureaucracy, empowerment of hiring any high qualified employees to get the job done, and a relatively better fit between specific staffing vendors and functional needs.

The disadvantages of local contracting can increase costs from non-standardization of hiring practices and procedures across the client form, a significant amount of word of mouth and subjective quality issues, high local costs and client firm us subjected to the capabilities of the staffing vendors and contract employees. However, local HR contracting is the most flexible, high quality, but expense, inefficient and ineffective HR outsourcing model for the client firm. Another model is the working period to be decided to outsource HR contracting. In this situation, in the short term and on a day-to-day basis, the client firm aims to achieve on economy of scale with its staffing vendors. The total costs of temporary workers as well as internal costs for contracting with several different vendors are higher than if it needs one staffing vendors to meet all its needs. So, the client company can set the reasonable pricing that it pays for its temporary outsourcing staffs. Each staffing vendor secures a different rate range with each vendor as opposed as one contact. In the long term, it is benefiting, each specialized staffing vendor is able to fully work with each function needs temporary utilization is better than the average. Mismatches are fewer. Functional departments are able to receive a high quality / high touch service in any time period. Another model is the centralizing is when the department standardizes the staffing process to drive costs down of temporary workers. This tends to occur when a percentage of non-core employees reach a certain ratio of core employees. The advantages include more uniform standards in hiring process, billing rates and pay rates, departmental hiring managers can refocus their effort to choose outsourcing staffing, criteria may be established for a performed suppliers list and greater security for the staffing established vendors that offer higher quality services. The disadvantages include new departmental responsibilities in HR which decreases outsourcing efficiencies for the organizations daily administrative direction is rather than long term strategic direction. Usually lacking qualifications to fulfill the responsibilities, overall, centralizing of HR outsourcing is that firms can achieve more standardization which additional bureaucratic costs and the necessary non-core jobs do not get done as a need. Another model is purchasing HR, which manages staffing vendors from HR to the purchasing unit of an organizations. The goal is to continue cost reductions by increasing efficiencies.

In conclusion, the main benefits of HR outsourcing include maintaining organizational control over the hiring process, application of purchasing capabilities for greater standardization in hiring processes pay rates and bill rates. So, any outsoucred HR organizations may be reduce hiring process cost.

Global outsourcing source strategy
in a value supply chain

What is global outsourcing source strategy in a departmental role? In a highly competitive global environment, many manufacturers are responded by setting and outsourcing relations for components and finished products with lower cost producers on a contractual electronic commerce department, (original equipment manufacturer basis). Outsourcing strategy is part of the value supply chain of corporate activated.

Nowadays, global outsourcing increases organizational and technological capacity of firms and cooperating a network of remotely located external suppliers performing. These understanding the important roles that product designers, engineers and production managers and purchasing manager etc. play in global sourcing strategy empowerment. Specially, electronic commerce is popular to supply chain. For example, Toyota car manufacturing company, owns unique capabilities by designing and manufacturing certain car components in-house , i.e. insourcing. Toyota also outsource manufacturing activities, Toyota adopts purchasing necessary, but no strategic inputs from independent component suppliers on obtaining a lower cost for these inputs. For example, products would be belts, tires and batteries to vehicle products that are not customized and do not differentiate its products from its competitors. Toyota's outsourcing strategy is car strategic inputs provide differentiation, e.g. engine, transmission etc. are sources from suppliers based on strategic partnership to gain to access to suppliers' capabilities and it is also a conceptualize global outsourcing sourcing strategy to Toyota car manufacturing company.

How value chain outsourcing affects firm level performance. Global outsourcing strategy means to identify which production units that will serve which particular markets and how components will be supplied for production and thus included a number of basic choices, companies can make in decision how to serve various markets. Either choice relates to the use of inputs, assembly or production within the country to serve a foreign market or decides to use of internal or external supplies of components or finished products. In this outsourcing source input situation, the term sourcing is needed to describe how multi-national companies mange in of components and finished products in serving foreign and domestic markets. Sourcing decision making is both contractual point of view, the sourcing of major components and products are occurred by multi-national companies. First is from parents or their foreign subsidiaries. Second is from independent suppliers on a contractual basis. The first type of sourcing is known as insourcing. Otherwise, the second type of sourcing is referred to outsourcing. How to achieve economies of scale by outsourcing or insourcing sourcing input strategy? Therefore, the two outsourcing strategies are multi-faceted and require careful examination.

Outsourcing benefits in economic view

The two economists (Abrahamson & Rosenkopf, 1993) indicated that In long term, outsourcing can help to reduce fixed investment in finance view point, in-house manufacturing facilities and thus lower the breakeven point, which subsequently helps boost an outsourcing company whose return on equity (ROE). Thus, if any one corporate performance is evaluated on the basis of its contribution to the company's ROE. Also, in the short term or long term on resource inputs outsourcing view, early adopters of outsourcing strategy indeed experienced efficiency gains as they were able to reduce fixed investment in in-house manufacturing facilities and lows their ROE. But, later adopters may have different to gain institutions legitimacy or because of competition pressures in the industry, despite some inherent uncertainties about the long term costs and benefits of outsourcing strategy. It seems that outsourcing strategy was devised as any organization's policy makers to access trade linkages of benefits for short term or long term.

Outsourcing strategy is a systematic analysis of the economic, political and regulatory implications indicates potential benefits along with a number of potentially negative side effects to any organizations. Then, outsourcing strategy will be caused this question: How to assess the risks and benefits of outsourcing for organizational sectors and nations both? The decision to change outsourcing behavior to carry a business activity may have profound implications for outsourcer and outsource receiver both, but little impact of the sector level. The common occurrence of industry decisions to outsource most manufacturing, including sale of factories, it created a new sub-sector, contract manufacturing. Otherwise, at a national level and public sectors become less distinct to outsourcing strategy. Public policy on outsourcing has stimulated extensive debate, privatization social justice and value for money etc. challenges.

II

What motivate outsourcing what is being outsourced risk and concerns

Whether what motivate outsourcing, evidence of what is being outsourced risk and concerns? Outsourcing activities include: outsources manufacturing components and other value adding activities. Some focused on employment is outsourced another firm's employees carrying out tasks previously performed one's own employees. Outsourcing is an activity outside the organization's chosen core competencies. It seems outsourcing is a sub-contracting relationships between firms, all foreign production, hiring of workers in non-traditional jobs, such as control workers and temporary and part time workers.

What are the motivations for outsourcing reasons? Why outsourcing is needed to any organization. For example, it can enable firms to focus on core activities. The concept of focus originates in operation on a small, manageable, number of tasks at which the operation becomes excellent to specific technologies and as a risk of vertical integration advantages. Other benefits of outsourcing appear is literature on strategic management, operations management, purchasing and supply and innovations. Moreover, outsourcing can improve flexibility to meet changing business conditions, demands for products, services and technologies by creating smaller and more flexible clear evidence includes improved creditability image, greater workforce flexibility and avoiding being backed into specific assets and technologies are harder to measure. How outsourcing can improve company performance. For airline manufacturing industry example, Hill & Jones (1995) showed that the manufacture of a large portion of the Boeing 767 is Boeing's third largest commercial aircraft, which is outsourced to Japanese manufacturers, which include Fuji, Kawasaki and Mitsubish. As a result, only 10% of the value of the 767 Boeing is produced in-house. So, outsourcing is an attempt to enhance manufacturing air place industry competitiveness.

How can choose smarter outsourcing?

How can choose smarter outsourcing? Organizations hope to do sight options to save money, among themselves staff layoffs and a reduction of overhead costs, such as office space. Private companies have long outsourced in order to save time and money. During periods of economic growth, many organizations began to use outsourcing more frequently and staff workloads grew in proportion to increase budgets. Tasks such as conducting needs assessments, reviewing proposals, conducting site visits, monitoring and creating evaluations systems were increasingly given to outside contractors, consulting firms and independent consultants in the belief that external specialists could do the work more efficiently and effectively than company itself.

Nowadays, there is a growing stream of organizations need to research into the outsourcing of innovation activities within the innovation, management, marketing and economics disciplines. These organizations need to understand how with the outsourcing practice becoming more commonplace in their industry. However, their behaviors bring these two questions: Whether outsource or internalize innovation activities and the performance implications of this decision can support for both transaction cost and resource based arguments is examined with both theory bases showing substantial attention? Whether outsourcing innovation activities can lead to faster product development and cost savings? On advantages hand, it is possible that outsourcing may lead to higher costs and slower new product development. Further the technological uncertainty may have conflicting impacts on the outsourcing decision that are not yet well understand. When outsourcing product development has reduced costs and has proved speed to market. On disadvantages hand, outsourcing has also reduce product development time delays and higher quality concerns. Why to cause performance implications of outsourced innovation activities in transaction in cost economics and the resource-based view point? When outsourcing product development has been to reduce costs and has improved speed to market, outsourcing product development is not unlike other make or buy decisions. So, make vs buy decision is similar to logistic and IT outsourcing. Internalization of product development will be preferred when transaction costs are excessive. Otherwise, the market i.e. outsourcing will be selected when transaction costs are low. Transaction costs can include adaption, safeguarding and measurement costs. Adaption costs represent efforts to adjust contract to change conditions and are a result of environmental uncertainty. When a firm may have to revise on agreement with a partner company, this facing substantial penalties, due to an unstable market environments, the firm is likely to perform this function internally. Safeguarding costs characterize the costs of an outsourcing provider acting opportunities after investments have been made in the inter-firm relationship and are the result of transaction specific investment. Measurement costs include all expenses with confirming that contracts have been fulfilled passably. The contracting firm may face substantial costs to estimate quality for contractual services. When the sum total of these transaction costs is substantial, internalization will be favored.

What is environmental uncertainty factor?

Environmental uncertainty refers to unanticipated changes in circumstances surrounding an exchange in market uncertain and technological uncertainty. Market uncertainty is the fluctuation and unpredictability of demand. With respect to innovation projects, market uncertainty may cause frequent changes to the development, complications and adding expense to external contracting. These changes may necessitate renegotiation or cancellation of innovation contracts, which will likely carry prohibitive penalties (a term) transaction costs. These transaction costs promote internalization under high levels of market uncertainty. Otherwise, technological uncertainty environments, selecting market governance allows firms the flexibility to end relationship should technical requirements shift. It seems that market and technological external change factor will influence to benefits to any organizations to choose outsourcing strategy.

On the other side, outsourcing can bring this question: Whether the offshore outsourcing of information technology jobs choice is suitable to any IT organizations? Nowadays. The offshore outsourcing if IT jobs from the United States has been enabled by a powerful influence of global economic demographic and technological forces. In fact, many IT companies were drawn to offshoring outsourcing because of the need for programmers to fix the Y2K problem in the late 1990- year. It is shortages of US programmers. Other factors driving this phenomenon include the wage gap between the US and developing countries, e.g. China and India, advances in technology, labor availability, expanding foreign markets and foreign government incentives. The spread of the offshoring phenomenon from low skill manufacturing to high wage white collar service industry jobs reduces the country's IT jobs critics, it represents the mobility for many US workers who saw post-secondary education as the route to a higher standard of living. The offshoring outsourcing of manufacturing and service jobs from the US to lower cost foreign nations become a national issue in a very short time. The impact of offshore outsource on the information technology sector gives outsourcing potential loss of millions of jobs at all wage levels and the critical contribution is the IT sector to US productivity growth. However, decisions about the locations of manufacturing or service facilities reflect market forces key factors include the size of local markets, capital availability and costs, labor availability skill levels and cost, logistic issues, reliability and infrastructure and IT in particular relationships with research institutions. All these factors will influence the choice of offshore outsource IT jobs strategy top any organizations.

● Whether outsourcing will bring
what kind of work skills.

Whether outsourcing will bring what kind of work skills. Many employers choose outsourcing to employ employees. This core of our work is identifying trends which will transform global society and the global marketplace. How it influences our nature of work form health care to technology, the work place and human identity. A decade ago, workers worried about jobs being outsourced overseas. Today companies, such as Odesk and Liveops can assemble teams " in the cloud" to dosales, customer support and many other tasks. It seems outsoucring can influence many high technological job of changes. Global connectivity, smart machines and new media are just some of the drivers reshaping how we thank about work, what constitutes work and the skills, we shall need to be productive contributors in the future. As computer technology in the cloud will be used popularly to society. A signal is typically a small or local innovation that has the potenial to grow in scale and geographic distribution. A signal can be a new product, a new practice, a new market strategy, a new policy or new technology, such as online cloud computing files storage service method. It is an innovative social science method to computer users. However, this new computer files storage method influences outsourcing service of needs increasing. It will have key drivers and skills areas that will be most relevant to the technological workforce of the future.

It is estimates that by 2025 year, the number of Americans over 60 age will increase by 70%. The challenge of an aging population will come. What it means to age, individuals will need to rearrange their approach to their career, family life and education to accommodate their life plan. Increasing, people will work long past 65 age in order to have adequate resources for retirement. Multiple careers will be commmplace and lifelong learning to prepare for occupational change will see major growth. To take advantage of this well experienced organizations will have to rethink the traditional career paths in organizations, creating more diversity and flexibility. As the high technological cloud computing storage method is invented. Any organizations can save their files to the central cloud computer storage system website to save or find their files from website more easily. It will reduce their computer department expenditure and staff salary. So, outsourcing computer file storage service demands will be influenced to increase to any organizations as well as organizations will reorganize their computer department job nature to shape the kinds of social, economic and political organizations which inhabit. Outsourcing is a good solve method to assist organizations to pay cheap salary to employ many retired high age workers by contract or temporary or part time method to reduce their computer department's number of employees and the retired labors only need to pay cheap salary to learn how to use internet to help whose employers to save their files to their outsourcing computer storage service provider's central computer storage system every day efficiently. So, organizations do not need to employ many computer department staffs to avoid to pay much salaries to this computer department expenditure. They can choose outsourcing to pay cheap salaries to employ many retirement labors to assist them to do simple office storage job from internet channel efficiently and effectively. Hence, internet high technological innovation can influence office outsoucing of job duties increasing.

Whether domestic outsoucing in the America, what assesses trends and effects on job quality. Nowadays, US firms' use of contractors and independent contractors and its effect on job quality and inequality. Why firms choose contract out for certain functions and assess their predictions about likely impacts on job quality, stagnant wages, growing inquality and the deterioration of job quality are among the most important challenges facing the US economy today. Although any country's domestic outsourcing , firms' use of contractors, franchises and independent contractors any one of these factors is a potentially important influence to companies reduce compensation and shift economy risk to workers. However, the domestic outsoucing takes place on a much larger scale and effects many more workers than has been recognized ranging from low wage service workers, security guards, warehouse workers and hotel housekeepers to professionals and technical workers, such as programmers, health care technicians and accountants. These tends are part of structural change in the organization of production to influence quality of jobs and the nature of employment contract after outsourcing jobs are popular. The quality of jobs include wages, benefits, employee skills and training and mobility opportunities and job security as well as inequality across jobs. Domestic outsoucing concerns these issues: such as employment and labor law, the provision of health, pension and other workplace benefits. However, any companies choose outsourcing of employment reasons include, such as that it relates how management choices to pursue value added or cost focused strategies. Contracting out is difficult to define because a large part ot economic activity has always occurred through business-to-business transactions, as captured in macro-economic input-output models. Outsoucing job employment method can influence any one labor's individual quality of jobs. Usually, international companies choose the offshoring of work in global supply chains. Until recently, the domestic counterpart outsourcing employment method has grown supply chains to domestic or regional outsoucing employment.

What factors cause domestic outsourcing and whether firm decisions about what to retain in-house and what to outsource have changes over time. Some evidence suggests that firms have responded by focusing on their core competencies and outsourcing low value added tasks as well as higher value added specialized functions. Advanced technologies have facilitated this process by allowing firms to outsource entire functions ans more easily monitor contractors as well as employees who work, leading to new forms of networked production and rise of specialized outsouring employment firms. Domestic outsoucing influences the changes of job quality, benefits, hours, workload, job stability, schedule stability and occupational safety, health, incidence of wage theft and access to training and promotions. Predictions are less clear for job requiring professional or technicial or specialized skills or those that are outsourced to large and diversified outsourced contractors. Types of outsourced contracts include: suppliers or vendors of products, such as manufacturing inputs or services, such as business services or staffs service or staffing firms, franchisees and independent contract, such as freelancers, independent contracts or non demand platform outsourced workers. It is significant restructuring of domestic manufacturing supply chains will greater reliance on suppliers and subcontractors. In addition, the potential growth of on demand outsourcing work as well as other forms of job fragmentation. It causes this question: How outsourced workers are multiple forms of income generating work to achieve economic security and how outsourcing workers can build career across jobs and over time.

Firm in every sector of the economy contract with other firms as part of their production process, as do governmental entities. The functions that are outsourced vary widely. For example: human resources ans research and development functions, building services, recycling, regulation and compliance, accounting, credit card collection, call centres, mortage and check processing, information technology and data processing, logistics and transportation, machine maintenance, cable installation, food services, food processing, parts manufacturing and assembly, laundry and housekeeping etc. outsourced jobs causes.

Whether what business impact of outsourcing will be caused? Nowadays, IT outsourcing was clearly a part of an effective management strategy that the companies felt IT outsourcing strategy can bring to achieve positive results. Information technology outsourcing providing servicers will be predicted to provide services that is expected to raise over the next five years minimum. The companies demand clients expected benefits of IT outsourcing and determined that cost reduction, increased operation, efficiency and improved IT effectiveness. What are the impacts of outsourcing to influence better long-term improvement in the business performance? It is impossible to being benefits of significant reduction and lower growth in sellings, general and administrative expense to IT outsourcing company demand clients. Also, pre-existing corporate cultures are focused on business improvement to IT outsourcing company demand clietns. In the past researches, some economists indicated that points can be used to reflect the actual numbers increase or decrease in percent. However, their prior researches shows that prior to outsourcing, the annual growth in selling, general and administration expenses of eompanies in the study was already 4.2 points lower than sector medium. Moreover, within one to two years after IT outsourcing these companies improved even most. Annual growth in selling and general administrative expenses for them was 9.9 points lower efford to assist any IT outsourcing will have selling and administrative expenses for long term. Also, almost two-third of the companies studied outperformed in increased growth in return on asset two to three years after IT outsourcing commenced. Prior to outsourcing, the annual ROA growth rate for companies in the study ws 7.5 points lower than the sector median. After outsourcing, however these companies experienced 8.6 points higher median a substantial change of 16.1 points. Also, nearly two to third of the companies studied grew earnings faster than their peers. Two to three years after IT outsourcing, companies experienced an annual rate of growth in earnings 11.8 points higher than the growth rate of the sector median. Thus, it seems IT outsourcing can assist the IT outsourcing demand clients to reduce expenditure and to raise income both as the same time. Then, it will cause these questions to IT outsourcing demand clients. Is outsourcing influencing in an economic downturn to finance sector in the short term? Is the finance sector's renewed change for outsourcing just a temporary cost-cutting measure?

Will today's economic climate initiate long term financial and productivity gains? Whether what are benefits and disadvantages of outsourcing finance sector IT. I shall demonstrate why outsourcing open source software support and maintenance can be a good choice to start. Firstly when company plans to budget cuts expenditures, IT outsourcing is often the first choice. For example in 2003 year, Zurich Financial services' sprawling IT department consisted of more than 7,500 employees. After posting a record loss of 3.4 billion the year before, Zurich decided to cut down on in those staff and outsource nearly half of its IT work. Outsourcing has successfully cut costs by 45 percent and cut the number of in house IT staff by 60 percent. Here are some of the benefits that companies enjoy when they outsource information technology functions to competent, reliable vendors.

In fact, it can be too expensive to maintain, company's own information technology, especially during a recession. Fortunately, many IT functions can be easily and efficiently outsourced, positively impacting individual company's bottom line. Employee costs are much higher than just salary and benefits, keeping employees happy, productive and busy takes time, effort and money. Although, many IT staffs will be dismissed, it will increase the unemployment ratio in societies. But, moving an IT service out of house means financial organizations don't have to worry about technology refresh costs in the future. It also cuts down on human resources requirements, specialist IT service provides which can provide the newest technologies and deliver quality service more than company itself in house information provides are the most effective to develop and implement and upgrade their clients' software or the launch on a new platform, due to the expert's time is wasted on day-to-day duties for whose other IT outsourcing demand clients. However, instead of IT outsourcing service outsourced offshoring in that service sector, how economic impact to influence the outsourced offshoring country. For example, United States continues to run an international trade surplus in services. Many Americans are particularly concerned about the loss of skilled, well paid jobs in such fields as computer programming and accounting etc. positions. These jobs seemed relatively secure at a time when many manufacturing jobs were being cost to import competition. Similarly, telephone call centers, once viewed as an esonomic development opportunity in some areas, increasingly are moving low wage countries, such as India and the Philippines. Thus, offshoring raises many questions for policymakers and general public. For example, which service jobs will be affected most by import competition. What are the likely effects of service-sector offshoring on U.S.A. output, employment and our standard of living, such as America? Is offshoring really a problem that requires restrictive government actions or are other kinds of policies more appropriate to give Americans or other countries the highest possible living standard?

The term of offshoring refers to the relocation of jobs and production to a foreign country. The relocated jobs and production could be at a foreign office of the same multinational company or at a separate company located abroad. In constrast, the term outsourcing doesn't necessary imply that jobs and production are relocated to another country. The major outsourcing service jobs include human resource, accounting and information technology etc. in-house service jobs in large organizations. However, the loss of service jobs and factory production is caused by offshoring is diffuclt to measure. It is also difficult to determine the impact of offshoring on total services employment in the United States or other countries. International trade in services covers a wide range of industries and activites. For example, travel and transportation includes travel expenditures, passenger fares and frieght and port services, royalties and license fees cover transactions including patents, copyrights, trademarks and other intangible proprietary rights to use, produce or distribute products. Other private services include many of these industries, such as education, financial services insurance, telecommunications and other professional services etc. Some economists indicated that occupational employment statistics for the Unisted States provided additional evidence that past service sector offshoring had been small. About 14 million service jobs were at risk of offshoring in 2000 year, when about 96 million service jobs had a low risk of ofshoring. The decline in the at-risk service occupations from 2000 year to 2002 year was about 218,000 jobs or roughly 109,000 jobs annually, relatively small number that is consistent with the estimates of McCarthy or Zandi. In percentage terms, employment in the at risk occupations fell at a faster rate from 2000 year to 2002 year than in the low risk occupations. This faster decline is consistent with offshoring activity, although the decline is consistent with other explanations as well, such as faster of technological change in industries employing the risk occupations or greater cyclical sensitivity in these industries. Because offshoring was not the only cause of job loss in the risk occupations, the number of jobs moved offshore was undoubtedly less than 109,000 jobs annually. However, the estimates may understate the total impact because domestic companies with expanding worldwide employment may have located may of their newly created jobs abroad even when they didn't reduce their US employment. Some of those foreign jobs might provide services to US customers and potentially foreign jobs might provide service to US . Conversely, the estimates may overstate the total job loss from offshoring of the foreign outsourcing of some support jobs prevents the loss of other domestic jobs by keeping US firms competitive in world markets. For example, cost reductions from offshoring IT jobs might help a US financial services company win foreign contracts, preserving many professionals and support jobs in the US.

Lower production costs in foreign countries are a major cause of service sector offering. Although, the costs of land and other resources may be cheaper abroad, but the main difference betweeb the US and developing countries is labor costs. There is a large gap in computer programmer wages between the US and other countries. Any organizational capital includes both physical capital, such as machinery and computers and human capital , such as skills and knowledge. The cost savings is come from offshoring also might be reduced if the firm needed to pay higher transportation and telecommunication costs or management spends more time on service quality and data security. Still, the much lower levels of wages ans benefits in developing countries suggests that many services can be produced abroad at lower cost. The in-house professional relocation of labor-intensive service activities, such as legal transcription services to countries with lower labor costs is consistent with economists' basic theory of international trade, comparative advantage. So, in-house outsourced professional service will be a corporative advantage, if the country's legal profession is poor level to compare with the another country. e.g. the skill in-house the legal professional labors of the developing country, such as China is poor educational level to compare with the developed country, such as US. So, if China large organizations chose to outsource themselves in-house legal service jobs to outsource offshoring to US legal professional lawyers to do. It can bring comparative advantage to China large outsourced in-house legal service organizations, due to these China outsourced large organizations can reduce to employ to pay too much salaries to these many in-house Chinese domestic lawyers and the US outsourced legal consultants whose can give more professional legal recommendation to serve to the China large organizations.

In conclusion, although offshoring strategy can increase unemployment chance for this disadvantge. But, all of outsourcing benefits weighs are more than the offsourcing disadvantages. However, outsourcing strategy can have these benefits to the outsourced service demanders. Such as outsourcing is no longer just about cost saving, it is also a strategic tool that may power the twenty first century global economy. Moreover, outsourcing can increase productivity and competitiveness, e.g. for every 1000 jobs British Airways sends to India , the airline saves $23 million, companies can devote a portion of their outsourcing savings to helping employees make job transitions, also leader can no longer afford to view outsourcing as a business tactic, it is now essential to remain competitive. On the world stage, workers now compete globally, so individuals must continually learn more to vie successfully with their peers worldwide, the average company only spends about 20% of the value of its outsourcing contracts to manage its relationship with the outsource provider. So, in the positive view point, outsourcing strategy can bring a potential primary driver of the global economy development. Although, outsourcing can also cause the raising of domestic unemployment chance. But companies may soon be more outsourced than in sourced, signifying a fundamental reorganization that will affect employees, managers, customers and executives. Customers' choice will increase product costs will drop and workers' roles will change. Finally, the most important, the developing country will earn comparative advantage from the developed country's employers' offshoring jobs provision. Thus, the developing country's unemployment rate will be reduced, then the global economy will be kept more balance fairly.

What are global competition influences?

Globalization brings international trade dramatically in recent decades and flows of products and services are important for achieving economic growth in development countries. However, in parallel with increasing global interconnections, progress toward world poverty is at the center of global development policy and research. Whether the super rich country, America can control globalization to influence wealth inequality. Despite the significant advancement in measuring poverty and income distribution which is limited to regard the impact to different economic policy both national and international on poverty outcomes. So whether can global competition influence wealth inequality in the world?

The super rich America which had been achieving foreign direct investment flows typically follow trade liberalization to different Asia countries, e.g. China. It invested to build many factories in China to employ cheaper China domestic labors to substitute to build factories to employ America domestic labors in America. The reason is because the China foreign labors of costs can be reduced very much to compare to employ America domestic labors for long term for America any businesses. Although, it seems that it can reduce China unemployment ratio. But, it seems that it can influence wealth inequality, due to America employers choose not to employ many domestic manufacturing labors who had been working in their current employer to earn incomes to support their life in America. So, this suddenly unemployment changing will influence many America manufacturing labors can not find another kind of same jobs easily in America. Due to there are many skillful manufacturing workers supply, but there are not many manufacturers demand, so this suitation cause them to feel difficult to find the same kind of manufacturing job nature to work in America very easily. To conclude, America manufacturing labor unemployment ratio will be raised. Moreover, many America manufacturing sectors of employers who need to pay much wages to China manufacturing labors, the America wealth will transfer to China to raise China GDP (Gross product production) income, per capita China individual manufacturing labor income. But, America the labor group's wealth will be reduced and the America GDP and per capita America individual income will be also reduced in society. I think the America employers' choice of foreign outsourcing employment issue will reduce America overall manufacturing labor individual wealth (capita per income) to be transferred to the other developing countries, e.g. China. It will cause China overall manufacturing labor individual wealth to be increased. So, it means that America employers' choice of foreign outsourcing employment issue will be influenced to America wealth inequality in itself country. Otherwise, it will influence China manufacturing labor group's wealth will be increased.

However, some economists indicate that the number of individuals living on less than USD$2.00 a day which can define poverty. In fact, some countries are encountering poverty challenge. For example, India still has many people whose have no more than USD$2.00 to support their living nowadays. So, it finds that income distribution is inequality or is equally conflicting in India.

Since 1980 year, America had become one developed country and its overall country economic growth or GDP income was the highest and per capital income or individual family income was also higher to compare other countries in the world. Otherwise, despite the relatively glowing of changing nature of income distribution to other developing countries. e.g. China, India which wealth inequality remains excessive until today. Even though, the debate on whether inequality has increased or has decreased over time remains unsolved, these developing countries' wealth inequality still remain high in the world. For example, the average levels of poverty head count and inequality in developing countries, e.g. India, China, Korea over 80 percent of the population is living at USA$2.00 a day to support their life, it means that who are poor to live in these developing countries.

In global competition, it includes that super rich country America anticipates, whether globalization will cause wealth inequality within and across nations, due to America anticipation. Supposing to the changes in per capita income are the main determinants of changes in poverty to wealth inequality in the world. But maximizing per capita income of fast global competition might not place sufficient weight on poverty and inequality reduction. The differences within and between countries inequality is an issue in the arguments on the impact of global competition. In special, America is the main player who decides to participate to global competition. Also, since 1980 year, America self country's economy had been beginning to grow high every year. Whether had America caused consequences to influence wealth inequality between other countries and within itself country income distribution, as well as poverty to cause wealth inequality in the world? Thus, to answer this question, it is important to confirm that it has relationship between poverty and wealth inequality and global competition to judge whether America can influence wealth inequality in the world finally. So, it seems that either the super rich country America can not influence wealth inequality in the world if it has been confirmed to have no any relationship between poverty and wealth inequality and global competition, due to America decides to participate to global competition. Otherwise, or America can influence wealth inequality in the world if it has been confirmed to have any relationship between poverty and wealth inequality and global competition.

Whether has it relationship between global competition and wealth inequality and poverty?

A key issue in the debate about global competition in general is the extent to which economic growth reduces poverty. If economic growth is to benefit everyone proportionally, the incomes of the poor would grow at the same rate as mean income. However, if economic growth in poverty reduction will be less(or more) depending in whether the incomes of the poor grow by less(more) than average. For example, Hong Kong, China, India, those developing countries still have many people (householders) are living of the poverty line, who do not earn enough income to support their families' living every day. Although, these countries' governments have social welfare to assist them and these countries seem their GDP incomes are growing up every year. But it is not enough to support them because the inflation will be raised every year for long term as well as there are many poor people are living in the poor housing environment due to who have not effort to pay rent or to buy house, no enough education fees to support them children to go to school to study between primary and tertiary stages, no enough saving to prepare retirement.

Whether it has the linkage between global competition and poverty to cause these developing countries' wealth inequality in the world. We can focus on two measures of global competition's trade and international capital flows. Globalization produces both winners and losers among the poor in the world. In fact, some poor individuals are made worse off by trade or financial integration to get support as income support from the governments, e.g. corn farmers in Mexico, China, food aid in India, China and other appropriately design social safety nets to accompany trade reforms. Also, America had been anticipating to global competition, it had affected different aspects of poverty in developing countries. It seems America's anticipation to global competition will be raised the openness growth link by these factors mobility such as related changes in global markets and power structures, changes in relative products and factor prices, changes the nature of technical progress and the technological process, changes terms of trade, affecting both the demand for exports and supply capacity, impact on the flow of information, global disinflation, i.e. the decline in inflation across countries' influencing the developing countries, e.g. Hong Kong, China, Korea, India etc. and developed countries, e.g. England, France, Germany, Japan, New Zealand, Australia etc. To mediate the effects and various channels to link global competition and income distribution poverty. It seems wealth inequality and poverty both are caused by global competition between developed and developing countries. If they have had direct relationship, whether the super rich country America had participated global competition between developing and developed countries in these different sectors , such as international trading, space science, medical science, weapon production etc. Has it enough ability to influence these countries' wealth inequality? In the another view point, these countries would not encounter wealth inequality if America did not participate the global trade competition. We need to judge the wealth inequality would not be caused if the global competition was only between the developing countries and the developed countries which particpate, excluding the America's participation.

In the history, economic inequality had been increasing in much of the industrialized world, but United States is unusual in the relatively high levels of inequality and the power reserved to its subnational governments. Using power resources framework, America government has ability to enact policies to reduce wealth inequality in itself country. However, some economists see inequality as a natural product of a market economy that is unimportant relative to outcomes like economic growth and poverty, when others see wealth inequality as a social ill in itself. So, it seems America had no any ability to cause wealth inequality issue occurrence to other countries before the industrialization stage passed. Although, it seems that America employers' choice of outsourcing foreign manufacturing labor strategy will influence itself country's manufacturing labor individual per capita income reduction to cause income inequality in itself country. But it is not represent that America had ability to influence wealth inequality to influence the world after it was one main player to participate the global competition in possible. So, it seems that the world's wealth inequality challenge is not influenced by America's participation to global competition when it was also one main player for the reason. Also it seems that the America's participation to global competition is not the main factor to cause these countries themselves wealth inequalities. It ought have other factors to cause the wealth inequality in the world. I shall indicate some of other factors which can influence wealth inequality in possible, such as below:

Is outsourcing the factor influence wealth inequality?

In the first view point factor is such as the extreme inequalities in incomes and assets has been caused to developed and developing both countries. For example, developed countries, e.g. France, Japan, Australia, England etc. developing countries, e.g. China, Hong Kong, Korea, India etc. These countries' employers had paid whose high level of management staff salary is very high and this management level of staff salary will be increased every year. Otherwise, these countries employers also paid whose middle and low both levels staff are very low and these both levels staff whose salary won't be increased very easily every year, even, they will be unemployed if their employers faced financial challenges.

Moreover in general, developing or developed countries which governments like to raise salary to the high management level public servant staffs easily. Otherwise, which won't like to raise salary to low or/and middle both levels public servant staffs every year easily. So, it will cause the public servant staff range is very high between the management level public servant staff and the low and middle levels public servant staff and any of these countries' government had done the unfair public servant salary review to treat to their low and middle level staffs in their countries every year for long term. It seems that America's participation to global competition will not influence any one of these countries' wealth inequality directly. So, it seems that the unfair salary review and wealth inequality of treatment issues will be caused to any one country in the world, even the global competition will not be caused, due to America's participation. So, it seems that any country's employers' outsoucing strategy which will influence unfair salary review and it will be one factor to influence the wealth inequality to themselves' employees.

In the another view point factor, I also argue the relationship between development countries and gender inequality why which can be explained by the process of development and society-specific factor to cause the wealth inequality by themselves. For example, China and India that have many people are poor today or at least some of them have cultural features that exacerbate favoritism toward males. Being poor is insufficient to explain parent's strong desire to have a son in China and India in custom. In past, the effects of gender inequality can influence economic development to these any of developing countries. More gender inequality causes wealth inequality in these any one of countries, e.g. China, India. In fact, poor countries have no a monopoly on gender inequality. Men earn more than women in essentially all societies. However, disparities in health, education and bargaining power within marriage tend to be larger in countries with low GDP per capita.

Moreover, the education gender inequality is also be caused to these poor countries. A negative relationship between the schooling gender gap and GDP is also for primary, secondary and tertiary school enrollment stages. Such as the male student enrollment number is often more than the female student enrollment number of primary, secondary and tertiary schools to these any one of countries, such as China, Korea, India every year.

So, these poor countries' male gender graduate students' income and male gender student enrollment number will be higher than the female gender graduate student's income and female gender student enrollment number every year for long term. Due to the high education graduates of the male gender is more than the female gender to these any one of countries every year. So, it will cause high wealth inequality between male and female graduate gender in these countries. It means that male average salary will be higher than female average salary in these countries, due to the male student enrollment number will be high than female student enrollment number in order to cause the male graduate student number will be higher in these countries every year. It seems that these countries' gender inequality factor can cause the male and female themselves income inequality, then it can cause male and female wealth inequality in these countries. So, it seems that it has no any relationship between the America's overseas outsourcing strategy participation to global competition and the gender inequality to cause wealth inequality to these countries.

To conclude, the causing of the world's wealth inequality's main factor is not come from the America's outsourcing strategy participation to global competition. It ought be the other both factors, such as themselves gender inequality factor and these countries themselves employers and governments unfair and unreasonable salary review factor which influence the wealth inequality to themselves, due to outsoucring strategy achievement. However, due to US encouraged outsourcing strategy to achieve to global businesses development in popular. Moreover, many global businessmen choose to dismiss their employees, then which let outsourced providers to help them to choose the suitable outsourced employees to do any company internal departments' job. So, outsourcing can also cause large number of unemployment. It will raise the upper managment and low(floor) labors their income distance very much. For long term, the global wealth inequality will be rasied. Hence, outsouring is the main factor to cause global wealth inequality.

Outsourcing educational development strategy

III

Human development policy

Human development policy is belong to educational strategy. The current economic crisis has affected all aspects of life resulting in political instability, personal financial troubles and a growing number of business bankruptcies. How to use effective human development educational policy to prevent the economic crisis threats. I shall indicate that governments ought to consider these different aspects of human development educational strategy to prevent the economic recession crisis occurrence to threaten to influence whose social economic growth.

On the human development educational strategy hand, examples of which include high quality education and health systems aspects. Different country's government ought to concern, due to it can support the productivity of an economy by providing healthy and highly trained individuals. Because of the country has good human development strategy, then it can use talent labors to assist its economic growth and good governance practices by governments easily. It seems that human development educational strategy, good governance and economic growth has close relationship, so it can reduce the economic recession during times of crisis occurrence. It means that human development can influence economic growth. Economic development implies both the improvement of people's health education and general well being and the presence of positive economic indicaties, such as economic growth and low unemployment with economic development, people will have better education and healthcare and be more productive. Better human development nations tend to have lower crime rates and greater political strategy than less human development nations.

Whether is it a consequence of human development educational strategy to prevent economic recession? It will be an important resource to influence economic growth. How does this human development public educational policy solve economic crisis? Can government use fiscal policy, such as human development to assist economic stabilization to promote growth and the increase of the capital income efficiency? A key issue relates to the effect of how to use public expenditure and its financing to spend human educational development on effects of fiscal policy by using a time series approach.

A general model that includes expenditure on education and health, which influences human capital, expenditure and health administration, public investment and transfers and consumption of public products four kinds of expenditure. The model can be used to explore and impact of human development expenditure is used on long run per capita income. So, the public expenditure on the long run per capita income can be explored for low, lower, middle and upper-middle income countries policy that is needed to be esimated how to spend for each aspect of human development expenditure to assist to every country's economy development.

What is time series perspective on economic growth to pursue for growth and human development strategies.

A time series perspective on economic growth may be more useful to pursue for growth and human development strategies. A time series can allow to pursue time series studies for particular countries or country groups at particular stages of economic growth. It can allow for a more specific micro behavior of economic agents. In general, any country has three income groups, such as low income, lower-middle income and upper middle income groups.

Also, any country may have these four types of public expenditure for human development which including: enhancing education and building up of human capital, public investment to finance general market and subsistence production, e.g. transportation system, such as roads, bridges, harbors, water supply, sanitation, health and care and education.

A 2005 year study had been carried by Dimonson, Marsh & Staunton, which performed an analysis is stock returns in 53 countries, going back to 1900 year for 17 countries, did not find evidence of a significant long term positive relationship between GDP growth rates and equity returns. Also the analysis from Schroders Economics team found that over the past sixty years, there has tended to be a positive relationship between GDP growth and equity market returns during the recovery, expansion and slowdown phases of the traditional business cycle.

This relationship has traditionally broken down during the recession phase. The Schroders economics team also indicated a traditional business cycle model, which has four stages. In the beginning, it is slowdown stage. It means output above trend, growth decelerating and inflation rising. Next is recession stage. It means output below trend, growth developing, inflation falling. Then, it is recovery stage. It means output below trend, growth decelerating, inflation falling. Finally, it is expansion stage, it means output above trend growth accelerating, inflation is rising.

The economic team also suggested the traditional business cycle model: In the slowdown stage, GDP growth is positive, but falling, inflation is high and rising, so policy strategy is tight recommended in the recession stage, GDP growth is negative and falling, inflation is falling. So, policy strategy is loosening recommended. In the recovery stage, GDP growth is negative and rising, inflation is low and falling, so policy strategy is loose recommended. Finally, the expansion stage, GDP growth is positive and rising, inflation is rising, so policy strategy is tightening recommended. It seems that governments ought concern the business cycle period to evaluate themselves country GDP growth to achieve the most effective policy to adopt to achieve different human development educational (strategies)policies to invest to present economic recession crisis occurrence. Usually, in the recovery and expansion phases of the business cycle, the stock market tends to perform well as rising GDP and earnings growth drives positive excess returns on equity. In the slowdown phase, inflation is still high and monetary policy remains tight, resulting in difficult environment for corporations. It can reduce earnings and stock valuations tends to result in negative excess returns for equities: declining GDP growth is therefore usually matched with poor equity performance. It also explained that during the recession phase, there is often GDP growth is falling, but the excess return on equity tends to be positive. Historically, falling inflation and an accompanying loosening of monetary policy is needed to rise re-rating.

Thus, it seems the business cycle and human development educational policy has close relationship. During in the slowdown stage, GDP growth is positive, but falling, inflation is high and rising, then the country's government ought spend less expenditures to human development because GDP growth is stable growth. Otherwise, during it is recession stage or recovery stage, it means output below trend, growth developing, inflation falling.

Then the country's government ought spend more to invest to any human development needs to prepare to raise whose labor productivity and GDP growth. Finally, during the expansion stage, GDP growth is positive and rising, inflation is rising. Then the country's government can spend less expenditures to invest human development. Thus, any country's government ought concern what is whose country's business cycle stage to arrange to spend more or less expenditures to achieve its human development educational policy in different business cycle stages.

What is quantitative evidence to review human development educational policy to reduce the threats from economic recession risk occurrence.

Nowadays, political scientists began to apply quantitative methods to classify and measure human resource educational and outsourcing strategy interactions. In general, any countries' policies that maximize growth are optimal that cares solely about pure " capitalists

I shall indicate how to apply quantitative evidence to review educational and outsoucing policy to reduce the threats from economic recession risk occurrence. In fact, economic or welfare outcomes to changes in regulatory policy has close relationship to be suggested outcome indicate to reduce risk face economic recession occurrence to any countries. Every country government ought design to gather quantitative data to prepare any outsourcing human educational development or/and outsoucing policy implementation to support mutual learning and best practice in different societal and market conditions. The goal is to help countries to build better government systems and implement policies at both national and regional level that lead to sustainable economic and social development.

The critical public policy challenge is to ensure that the expected economic benefits from regulatory changes are both achieved and outweigh any economic cost imposed. I shall indicate evidence on the outcomes of regulatory policies to help policymakers how design regulatory measures that work better. This method is called "regulatory management". This regulatory management study suggests some conclusions to any policymakers. Firstly, poorly designed human development or/and outsoucing policy regulation can not raise economic activities and ultimately reduce economic growth. Secondly, it is impossible between a regulatory human development or/and outsoucing policy change and the impact on economic outcomes, such as economic growth is from statistic method easily. Third, the reliance on economic recession analysis to investigate the relationship across countries between regulatory variables and economic outcomes may not be readily applicable to any countries and may not always be expressed in economic values. It is particularly useful in developing countries regulatory human development and/or outoucing policy measures for recommendation to policymakers only. Fourth, most quantitative studies deal with the costs of human development and/or outsourcing strategy regulation and give little or no attention to quantifying the benefits of regulation.

For the policymaker, it is important to compare the estimated costs of human development and/or outsourcing regulation. Any policy regulation is intended to correct market failures and assist to economic efficiency and growth. The public policy aims to reduce socially unacceptable income and wealth distributions or it can satisfy expectation that the public should have access to certain products and services, e.g. health care and education irrespective of ability to pay, such as merit products. Some of human development or/and outsoucing strategy regulation, that governments need to concern, e.g. of property rights, company law, law of contract etc. and regulation can provide important economic and social, including environmental benefits. Of course, those benefits need to be set against the costs. Because regulations are the operations of effective economies and societies to market rules, firm's outsoucing and human development strategy e.g. law of contract and protecting property rights and the rights of citizens. It seems regulatory management is important to influence any policies can be achieved effectively, due to one good regulation can supervise the firm leader's behavior and otherwise one bad regulation can not supervise the firm leader's behavior, even it can not assist the country economic growth for long term. So, any firm leader needs to concern how to use quantitative evidence to review human development or/and outsoucring strategy policy if who hopes whose policy's regulations are achieved effectively.

At the same time, economic, environmental and welfare pressures raise the demand for regulation above minimum needed for operating a market economy to prepare to face the economic recession occurrence. So, evidence on the outcomes of outsoucing and/or human development strategy regulatory policies should help policymakers design regulatory measures that work better. Similarly, evidence on the success or failure of regulation can be used for public accountability purposes. Regulatory human development or/and outsoucring strategy policy is defined as the process by which government, when identifying a policy objectives, decides whether to use regulation as a policy instrument and proceeds to draft and adopt a regulation through evidence based decision making. The human development or/and outsoucing strategy shall commit governments to remain a regulatory management system, articulating regulatory policy goals, and the impacts of regulation on competitiveness and economic growth. For example, one firm human development and/or outsoucing strategy regulation, such as employment law or competition law, the regulation of employment law is applied to control any employers' behaviors to give the fair treatment to whose employees and to protect employees' benefits. Besides the regulation of competition law is applied to control the fair competition in market.

Why this human development and/or outsourcing strategy regulations has direct relationship to economy growth. An identifiable economy theory of specific regulatory policies, e.g. administrative simplification and specific economic and welfare outcomes, e.g. high economic growth. The result is a series about the impact of regulatory management on economic indicators. There can be set out as a causal. Thus regulation can be supportive of market transactions and may result in significant economic, social and environmental benefits. At the same time, ill-designed regulation can have appreciable economic costs, leading to the concept of regulatory burden. In particular, good regulation can reduce the chance of lower economic growth or GDP occurrence, damage investment and competitiveness. But, it has also weakness, such as regulatory costs may act as a barrier to entry into industry in the form of set up cost, e.g. installing equipment to meet health and safety laws and on going annual cost, e.g. preparing returns and facilities inspections.

However, human development and/or outsourcing strategy regulatory can be unduly costly to comply with administrator and enforce, but it simplification can reduce the regulatory burden. For example, regulation may not only affect the behavior of those targeted by a rule (direct effects), but invoke behavioral change in the economy (indirect effects). Whether regulation can support governments to avoid or reduce the threats of economic recession occurrence, it depends on the firm leader's concern how to use quantitative evidence to review human development and/or outsourcing strategy policy before who decides to implement which kinds of regulatory management methods.

In recent year, some countries' firms and/or governments had considered how to achieve human development and/or outsourcing strategy policy field with a view to introducing better regulation. The aim is to ensure that regulation occurs only when it does improve social welfare and that regulatory changes do, so with the minimum net cost or maximum net benefit to society. For a policy making perspective, it is important to appreciate how and why a regulatory achievement can be expected to result in a particular impact.

Causal chain analysis is a technique for explaining the way in which a caused regulatory results in an economic impact. By helping to understand the how and why questions of the firm which needs to decide outsourcing and/or human development strategy, regulatory impact, so causal chain analysis can provide policymakers, with relevant information on the consequences of their policy decisions. It seems that human development and/or outsourcing strategy regulation can lead economic improvements, such as higher GDP growth, higher productivity, move business start ups. etc. Due to the causal chain analysis relates to each component separately. So, any decision maker hopes to achieve better regulation, who needs time to attempt to different regulations to achieve whose policies every year. Then, who can review why whose policy can not improve whose country's economic growth as well as to attempt to find reasons how to apply better human development and/or outsoucring strategy regulatory to achieve better policy to improve its country's economic growth. It seems review regulatory policy which ought to concern to any decision maker, if who wanted to achieve better regulatory policy to raise economic and welfare gains every year.

In capitalism view, capitalism tends equal systematically, through not uniformly to reward business behaviour ,such as human development and/or outsoucing strategy that is honest, fair civil and compassionate. When does irrational honesty behaviour influence social economy development? It concerns behavioral economy to individual decision maker whose individual psychology, social psychology into economics. It helps any organization's human development and/or outsoucing strategy policy makers to incentive in market transactions and in response to policy interventions. So, policy advisers are already using the finding of behavioural economy to advantage to public policy, there is nothing about behavioural economy, but for a long time, it has tended to be concerned how the social economic development, particularly in macroeconomy. For example, human development and/or outsourcing strategy policy makers concern of money in nominal rather than real terms in whose how to solve to unemployment. Also, policy makers neglect to recognize how economic motivations apart from those based on rational calculation usually. Most, probably of policy decision makers' decisions to will be drawn out over many days to come, who feels action rather than inaction to any decision immediately, and not as the outcome of a weighted average of probabiities. It seems that the policy decision maker's irrational honesty behaviour will influence how our social's economic development to be good or bad.

Regulatory management method

Whether it has relationship between human development and/or outsourcing strategy political instability and national economic performance. By past history indicated that the depletion of resource ,e.g. human resource and/or business strategy during wars may be one reason why some countries fail to sustain adequate economic growth. However, because economic growth affects a population's well being, this question concerning how was related to growth is important from a policy perspective. So, civil wars can influence any country's economic growth because civil war can cause the falling changes in a country's physical and human capital as well as lacking technology supporting can reduce GDP per capita to be country during war occurs. For example, during civil war does not occur, then trade liberalization, democracy, government stability and a legal system that strongly protects private property rights enhance growth.

Finally, I shall explain why human development behavior, such as honesty has moral consequences to cause economic growth. For citizens of all too many of the different countries, where poverty is still the normal. But the tangible improvements in the basic of life that make economic growth, so important whenever living standards are low, greater life expectancy, few diseases, less infant mortality and malnutrition have mostly been played out long before a country's per capita income reaches the levels enjoyed in today's advanced industralized economy. In fact, immoral or dishonesty business or economic behaviours, such as wrong outsourcing strategy achievement are caused by some business leaders who pursue material well being and who aim to do benefit to themselves, but it will cause illegal money transactions to raise any overall country's economic or GDP growth. In fact, this business transactions are not legal. So, which can't cause GDP or economic growth to any country. Also, the illegal businesses can not contribute any benefits to any society, so which can not bring any economic benefits or welfares to any countries to satisfy any citizen'e needs ensurely. Even, in parts of the world where the need to improve nutrition and literacy and human life expectancy is urgent, there is often aspect to the recognition that achieving superior growth is a top priority. So, it seems dishonesty human development behaviours will not improve and raise low income level people whose life expectancy and life quality because this illegal businesses income is used to spend to the illegal businesses or immoral policy decision makers themselves benefits and who won't spend to social welfare. It seems that these illegal businesss or immoral policies can not assist any economic growth and raise GDP growth rate as well as dishonesty or immoral economic activities can not bring any benefits to societies in our world, even these bad behaviours will bring harm to our societies. e.g. encouraging illegal drug sale to harm young people health and raising crimes rates; winning illegal gamble to earn illegal profit to increase high interest loan businesses and crimes or causing bad families relationship to raise social challenges.

What is the root of the irrational behavioural problem? I believe that is our conventional thinking about economic growth fails to reflect the breadth of what growth, or its absence, means for any society. There are some people's dishonest behaviours only weigh material positives against moral negatives. I believe this dishonest economic activites are seriously. In some cirsumstances dangerous incomplete, the value of arising standard of living lies individuals live, but in how it shapes the social, political and ultimately the moral character of a people. It seems any organization's wrong human development behavior or wrong outsourcing strategy will influence the country's economy growth.

Economic growth means a rising standard of living for the clear majority of citizens. So, dishonest economic behaviours can only give benefits to the individual and these irrational behaviours can not give welfare to overall societies. In fact, economic growth bears moral benefits as well. So, it seems dishonest behaviours can not raise moral benefit, then it can not also raise economic growth to any country. Moreover, dishonest behaviours are also caused to any country's political democracy. e.g. Many policy decision makers usually only consider self benefit, so who will neglect to consider social welfare benefits to whose citizen. Themselve benefit behaviours will be unfair to whose citizen. The importance of the connection between economic growth and social and political progress and the consequent concern for what will happen of living standards tail to improve, are not limited to the United States and other countries that already have high income and established democracies. So, economic growth or its absence often plays a significant role not only progress from dictatorship to democracy, but also the democracies by new dictatorships.

Also, for dishonest behaviours are caused by decision makers, such as the link between economic growth and social and political progress in the developing countries has yet other political implicatons as well. For example, the continuing absence of political demoracy and basic personal freedoms in China has deeply troubled many observers in the West. Until China gained admisson to the World trade Organization in 2002 year, these concerns regularly gave rise in the Uniter States to debate on whether to trade with China on a most favored nation basis. These concerns still cause questions about whether to give Chinese firms advantage advanced American oil company. Both sides in this debate share the same objective: to foster China's political liberalization. How to do so , however, remains the focus of intense disagreement. The improvement in nutrition, housing, sanitation and transportation has been dramatic, when the freedom of Chinese citizens to make economic choices, where to work, what to buy, when to start a business is already broader than it was with continued economic advance, the average Chinese standard of living is still only one eighth that in the United states, greater freedom to make political choices too, it will probably follow. So the economy is actually developing, like China won't have to wait until China can achieve Western level incomes before they experience significant political and social liberalization.

To conclude, if any country's policy makers who do not consider citizen welfare and who only consider self benefit, it will cause dishonest behaviours to influence social economic development to cause poor situation for long term. So, policy makers must need concern their behaviors are rational choice to make any economic decisions to let their citizen to give welfares for long term. Also any businessmen ought choose to do rational economic behaviours to benefits for societies and clients and governments in order to achieve economic growth to GDP to their countries if who hope whose businesses can be stable to compete for long term. So, policy decision makers and businesses ought consider rational honesty behaviour before who do any economic decision.

IV

Outsourcing educational development policy

How honesty is influenced to economic positive relationship? The dishonesty behaviour includes: e.g. corruption is as an illegal payment to a public agent to obtain a benefit that may or may not be deserved, or the abuse of public office for private gains to consume, corruption probably amounts are to a large share of the gross national product in any countries. So, corruption worries policy makers and international organizations, who remains the adverse effects of corruption.

However, in the macroeconomic view, the academic literature is less definite about how bribes minimize the waiting costs associated with queuing in a equilibrium. Both of those waiting cost associated with queuing and inefficiency models equate bribes as allocating the true worth of the licenses or permit to the most worthy bidder in public sector. Forbidding bribes that amounts to prohibiting the use of price mechanism in the public sector. In terms of economic growth, the only thing worse than a society over centralized, dishonest bureaucracy is over-centralized. So, the quality of government institutions, including the degree of corruption, affects investment and growth as much as other political economy variable. e.g. political freedom, civil liberties and political violence. Another example, some firms that pay more bribes also spend more time with bureaucrats in more corrupt countries and have a higher cost of capital, thus countering the view of corruption.

Finally, some countries are likely are fairer and regulation is less. How does corruption affect income inequality? In addition, capital market imperfection and government spending have been suggested as two channels for corruption to affect inequality and economic growth. Finally, to what extent can corruption explain the differences in inequality and economic growth? So, it seems corruption is associated with a smaller increase in income inequality and a larger drop in growth rates. Also, corruption raises income inequality to a lesser extent in countries to achieve higher government spending. So, it seems corruption dishonest behaviour has close relationship to influence any countries' GDP economic growth.

Corruption is understood as sale of government property for private gain. However, most economists view corruption as a major obstacle to development. It is seen as one of the causes of low income and is believed to play a critical role in poverty. Perhaps the most quoted example of this is speed money paid by business people to government officials to speed up bureaucraties procedures. At the macro level, there is evidence that corruption affects adversely many of the proxy causes of economic growth. e.g. investment in manufactured and human capital. Moreover, high levels of corruption tend to with a lack of political accountability and disrespect for property rights factors which themselves tend to be obstacles to economic growth. More fundamentally, however, there is a sense in which the focus on growth in GDP per capita is misguided.

Ultimately, human educational development is about how to improvement in human welfare. However, corruption is developing a few with access systematic distort political and economic decisions which might be made systematically with conflict of interest at play. For example, different countries' banks which achieve different bank schemes to aim to avoid illegal money saving from drug trafficking to cause false economic growth in any countries. The anti-corruption strategy advocated to cconomic development, democratic reform a strong civil society with access to information and overseeing the state, and the presence of rule of law. The governance program facilities at the request of client governments, a series and surveys involving broad segments of society and national and local government performance.

The causes of its human educational development and many and vary from one country to the next. It seems corruption dishonest behaviours can cause to seem as one country's false economy growth and even, global false economy growth after any illegal economic activities had been done from any illegal businessmen. So corruption is a global issue which is government all over the world. However, what is the causes and consequences of corruption? It is possible that corruption is the intentional with length relationship aimed at deriving some advantage from this behaviour for oneself or for related individuals. So, in micro-economic view, corruption cause is derived from some advantage from this behaviour for the person. Otherwise, in macro-economic view, corruption cause is also derived from some advantage this behaviour for the organization, even overall country's social benefit, e.g. illegal shares buying and selling trading activities, illegal bank saving transaction source from drug trafficking activities.

On human development educational aspect, many of the assumptions which are attempted to rationalize the process of educational development have been criticized or abandon. However, the education quality role of different educational regulation, the choice of financing methods, the examination and certification procedures or various other regulation and incentive structures will influence educational effect to satisfy public needs. Thus, educational policy makers need to satisfy public needs. Moreover, educational policymakers also need to concern any new policy making environment which will seriously constrain their attempts to ensure the early discussion of planning considerations as part of the education policy making process. So, every country's environment factor will influence every educational policymaker's individual decision.

As defined, policy represents decisions that are designed to guide (including to constrain future decisions or to initiate and guide the implementation of previous decisions). It is this time bound nature of policy and of policy making that makes it is such a critical concern for the educational planner. However, the failure of the traditional planning models and the recognition of the lack of nationality that can occur in policy making there combined to create an atmosphere of pessimism among some educationalists.

To capture the details of the decision making process of any educational planning itself, an analytical framework is presented that goes beyond the initial decision point to examine both the preceding actions (contextual assessment, technical analysis and the generation, valuation and selection of policy options) and the subsequent activities (planning and conducting implementation, impact assessment and where appropriate, design). Thus, the framework covers the full policy planning process, but with a focus on the facilitating and constraining effects that policy decisions and how they were derived and have no the choices available to educational planners.

There are two ways of value to educational planners. First, the methodology of the framework and conclusions of the any one of educational case studies should help in the analysis of current educational policies and decision making procedures (an analysis of policy). So, it is a present method to gather current data from current case studies to make the update conclusions to achieve any any of eductional policies. Otherwise, Second, the another framework can be applied to have evaluation of proposed policies and used to forecast policy outcomes and the probability of successful implementation, given the country of fiscal and management capacity, political commitment etc. So, this framwork is a futuer predict educational method to gather data how to get the recommedation to achieve the effictive quality of educational policy in the future.

Educational policies can be lower differ in terms of scope, complexity, decision environment, range of choices and decision criteria. Any educational policy decision deals with large scale policies and broad resource allocation will have these questions to need to answer. For example, on strategic view, how can we provide basic education at a reasonable cost to meet equity and efficiency objectives? On multi program view, should resources be allocated to university level education? On program view, how would occupational training centre be designed and provided across the country? On issue specific view, should graduated of rural universities be allowed to transfer to any one of city area universities to study easily? On the psychological view, some researches indicated behavioral economics with emotions has close relationship to any policy making, such as educational policy. More recently, economists as well as psychologists who are specifically interested in decision making have begun to take greater concerning emotional influence. So, it seems any policy decision making whose any one of final policy decisions which is influenced to achieve or not achieve from their emotion indirectly. Usually, then an economy is doing well, there is less incentive to encourage new entrepreneurial firms if the country's citizens and firms have enough jobs supply and have enough labor supply in the job market. It seems that good economic growth country will have this question why it needs to take a risk on something new. So, emotions have close link to our societies to influence any country's citizens real needs and entrepreneurs' business aim to develop any societies' economy to be grown. So, any countries' policies decision makers ought concern whose enterprises and citizens whose real needs, then who can attempt to choose what methods of policies to assist whose countries' economy development more effective.

What is national human development educational policy

However, behavioural economy is not concerned with such normal phenomena, rather it is concerned with consistent patterns of behaviour which depart from rational actor models. The mean may be displaced as when most people under-scare for retirement, or the distribution of behaviour may reflect several modes of behaviour as when users of credit cards who pay in full and those who pay minimum amounts. Otherwise, in terms of public policy, most such departures from rationality have little or no consequence. It is possible to accomodate non-rational behaviour with a set of indifference with a quality, such as non-rational utility, ensuring that all behaviour can be modelled. Concerning irrational honesty whether this behavior can influence social economic development. I shall indicate those questions to attempt to be considered, such as: Can there be a growing scaraity without a growing shortage or a growing shortage with a growing scarcity? Can a decision be economic if there is no money in involved? Can there be surplus food in a society where people are hungry? For example, building ordinary and building luxury housing both involves using many of the same resources, such as bricks, pipes, and construction labour. How does the allocation of these resources between ordinary housing and luxury housing tend to change after rent control laws are passed? When a government institution or program produces counter productive results, is that necessarily a sign of irrationality on the part of those who run that particular institution or program? Why do American manufacturers of computers or television sets tend to have them transported by others? When Chinese manufacturers tend to transport themselves? How did the movement of population from rural to urban America affect the economy of retail selling in the early twentieth century? Advertising even when it is successful, is often considered to be a benefit only to those who advertise, but of no benefit to consumers, who have to pay the cost of the advertisement in the higher price of the products who buy. Is it irrational economy behaviour to society? Why would luxury hotels be charging lower rates than economy hotels? Whether governments choose to protect competition or protect competitors which method is better? What have been some of the economic and social consequences of the substitution of machine power for human strength, as a result of industralization and the growing importance of knowledge, skills and experience in a high-technological economy? How can per capita income be increasing by 50 % over a period of years, when average family income and average householder income remain almost stable over those same year? Does inequality of income tend to be greater or less in long run than in the short run?

All above questions concern the social and economic influences won't be better if the policy decision makers or businessmen do any irrational honesty behaviours. It seems rational honesty behaviour is important to any policy decision makers or businessmen because whose rational or irrational behaviour can influence social economic development directly are driven to act by economic as well as social ethical and other reasons. So economists need to study of what motivates individual acts, especially regarding economic decisions, offers an intellectual challenge to the human sciences. So, if economists can predict to judge whether any policy decision makers or businessmen whose act is irrational or rational, then who can assist the country's economic development more easily.

On natural environment view, whether every country's natural environment has close relationship to assist its economic growth. The natural environment is central to economic activity and growth, providing the resources, we need to produce products and services and absorbing and processing unwanted by-product in the form of pollution add waste. So, environment assets contribute to managing risks to economic and social activity helps to regulate flood risks, regulating the local climate both air quality and temperature and maintaining the supply of clean water and resources both.

Government's role is to send clear signals and set a long term policy framework in order to provide businesses with the certainty who need to make investments in low carbon and resource efficient technologies. It is also essential that government listens to and works with business, so that policies are designed in a way that avoids unnecessary burdens and removes potential barriers to success. So, the natural environment plays an important role in supporting economic activity. It contributes: directly, by providing resources and raw materials, such as water, timber and minerals that are required as inputs for the production of products and services and indirectly, through services provided by ecosystems including carbon water purification, managing flood risks and nutrient cycling.

The relationship between economic growth and the environment education is complex. Several different drivers come into play, including the scale and composition of the economy, particularly the share of services in GDP as opposed to primary industries and manufacturing and changes in technology that have the potential to reduce the environmental impacts of production and consumption decisions when also driving economic growth. In fact, economic growth involves the combinations of different types of capital to produce products and services these include; produced capital, such as machinery, buildings and roads; human capital, such as skills and knowledge, natural capital, e.g. raw materials are extract from the earth, carbon and services is provided by forests and social capital, such as institutions and ties within communities. So, government needs to concern that national resources can not be extracted too much to lead our natural capital is lacked to produce any products or to provide services in the future.

In particular, market failure in the provision and use of environmental resources mean that natural assets would be over-used in the absence of government intervention. These market failures arise from the public product characteristics of the natural environment, external costs and benefits, where the use of a resource by one party has impacts on others, difficulties in capturing the full benefits of business investment in environmental research and development, and information failure.

Market failures may include water quality and to vehicle emissions to influence human's body health. So, any countries' government needs to achieve these policies which concerns on environmental protection aspect to achieve its public spending and technology policy, such as on developing flood infrastructure, supporting low carbon technologies electric vehicles. Also on the information provision and other policies to address barriers to influence consumer's behavior change, such as product labelling policies and policies to increase take up of resource efficiency measures to provide environment protection. So, effective environmental policy is likely to require and the use of multiple instruments, each tackling to require part of the problem when avoiding duplication and unnecessary regulatory burdens. Also, pricing environmental inputs can correctly help any businessmen to manage how to use natural resources effectively.

Environmental education policy aims to reduce how the economy and the businesses are to adverse environmental events, by reducing environmental risk both. For example, not just investments that facilities emissions reductions to avoid dangerous climate change, but also those investments that help to economy adapt to climate impacts already locked in by past and current emissions. The natural environment plays a key role in our economy, as a direct input into production and through the many services it provides.

Environmental resources, such as minerals and fossil fuels directly facilities the production of products and services. The environment provides other services that enable economic activity, such as carbon, filtering air and soil formation. It is also vital for against flood risk, and soil formation. It is also vital for our wellbeing, providing us with recreational opportunities, improving our health and much more. Human wellbeing in a complex and diverse concept, determined by a wide-range of factors including levels of income absolute and relative, health status, educational attainment, housing conditions and environmental quality.

National capital contributes to economic output through two main channels: directly as an input to the process of economic activity, indirectly through its effect on the productivity of the other factors of production. However, natural capital is as a direct input to wealth creation, which can provide the raw materials for economic production of products the raw materials for economic production of products and services, it includes non renewable resources like, fossil fuels, minerals metal extracted from the natural environment to produce energy, machinery, consumer products, renewable resources, natural processes or own reproduction. Why do our governments need to concern environmental policy? The reasons include natural areas provide global life support functions, including climate regulation and regulation of the chemical composition of the atmosphere and oceans. When natural areas play a role in the maintenance of life essential services, it is difficult to evaluate and demonstrate the contribution that particular habitat types or areas make. Water regulation can reduce flood and storm protection and prevent damage. Natural processes can also provide water quality benefits, pollution includes the removal of nutrients and pollutants from water, filtering of dust from the air, and providing noise. Waste sink includes all non recycled waste is produced by economic activity. In the absorptive capacity of the atmosphere, the oceans and the soil protection, such as many wetland habitats, provides benefits by preventing soil loss. Nutrient cycling includes storage, processing and acquisition of nutrients essential for plant growth in ecological process and waste decomposition, naturally occurring micro-organisms provide benefits through their ability to break down organization matter and speed up the process of waste decomposition.

Government overseas education outsourcing policy

As the global financial crisis has reminded as once again of the economic role of trust and confidence, social capital attributes which are difficult to influence any policy decision maker's ration decision making more easily. Referring to recent financial crisis, which is related to any psychological drivers of economy activity, we can not understand the economic developments of recent times without psychological insights which go beyond estabished notions of rationality in its economic sense. As peope with weigh the costs and benefits of each possibility. This assumption is based on the expectation that individuals and firms will act in a consistent manner, with a reasonably well defined notion of what who like and what whose objectives are, and with a reasonable understanding of how to attain those objectives.

In fact, behavioural economy is a complement to deductive processes based on those assumptions. In any discipline with practical applications, such as public policy, conclusion is reached by chains of deductive logic based on those assumptions require the test of falsifiability or refutability, or at least that they be supported by confirmatory evidence. However, a rational means the predictive validity of the rational model holds, but that doesn't mean achieving policy should ignore interventions. For example, most people rationally avoid self-harm, but there will be extreme tails of highly protective and of highly reckless behaviour: the latter may require specific protection. So, it seems it has relationship between global financial crisis and individual or organization's irrational behaviour.

How government overseas outsourcing policy can influence on capturing private investment. Can government overseas outsourcing policy can attract foreign direct investment or different countries? Increased levels of trade and foreign direct investment worldwide, a cause or effect of the closer interdependence of world economies are a reality. What is the relationship among these private, public and civil society sectors? Every country contribution is to add to the public policy stream to understand how the main forces in society operate and cooperate in promoting foreign direct investment. Governments have always been concerned about how to position themselves in an increasingly competitive market for a limited supply of investment resources. Why should a multi-national firm choose one country attraction ? e.g. tax breaks, profit repatriation, low domestic content requirement etc. How can one country strategically outsoucing position itself against others? Is there an association between pro-social public policy and levels of global private investment? We are particularly interested in those economies in earlier stages of development, where pro-social policies are a rarer phenomenon, as they provide a testing for our hypotheses. What is the relationship between the ability of an host country to attract private investment and the quality of pubic policies affecting the life of its citizens? Are pro-social host government policies in host countries linked to higher inward flows of foreign direct investment to that country?

There has three country level macroeconomic indicators to represent different facets of size: Host country economy growth rate, host country population and host country's rate of inflation. GDP growth, the annual percent change of output in real terms percent, reflects the strength of local economy and the increase in the size of domestic market, opening the door to large sales and high profits. Thus, higher GDP growth should generally be attracted to larger foreign investment. Population is another indicator of market size. It attracted to foreign investment with both large populations and high GDP per capita. So, encouraging immigration and birth rate can attract more foreign investment. Inflation enters the regression as a proxy for macroeconomic stability and as a reflection of the internal or external shocks suffered by the economy during the period under study, which may attract potential inflation sign of internal economic instability and of the host government's inability to maintain consistent monetary policy. It will influence foreign investment confidence. So stable inflation of the host country can increase confidence to let more foreign investment.

How fiscal policy can affect medium to long term economic growth. It is difficult to measure the factors and to determine causality with certainty, between fiscal policy and economic growth relationship. Fiscal reforms are needed to concern structural reforms, e.g. labor or trade and supportive macroeconomic policies. At the macro level, fiscal policy can help to ensure macroeconomic stability, an essential prerequisite for growth at the micro level, tax and expenditure policies can boost growth by altering work and investment incentives, promoting human capital accumulation and enhancing total factor productivity. For example, combining fiscal reforms, e.g. sealing up infrastructure investment when improving the public investment process can increase their effectiveness.

Complementary reforms, such as liberalizing trade of fiscal reforms by promoting savings, stimulating investment and not lacking productivity gains, policy uncertainty and high levels of public debt large fiscal deficits reduce aggregate savings in the economy and may lead to inflation, high interest rates and balance of payments pressures, with negative growth consequences. Policymakers need to concern the durability and equity. For example, Netherland, an expenditure cut of 15% of GDP between 1982 year and 2000 year created room sector job-creation. At the same time, both countries managed to avert adverse consequence on income inequality. In advanced and emerging market economies, age related spending on public persons and health care accounts for a large share of government spending (40% and 30%, respectively, IMF, 2014 f). Otherwise, Poland shifted from a financially defined benefit system to an actuarially solvent defined contribution system, and Germany put its pension system on a more sound financial by linking pension benefits to the old age dependency ratio, tightening access to early retirement and rising the statutory retirement age. In health care, Germany and the Netherlands introduced a combination of macro and micro level reforms to contain cost and enhance efficiency, including price controls on pharmaceuticals, higher co-payment and contributions and budget.

National leadership and educational productivity relationship

Whether national leadership and economic growth has close relationship. Leaders have strongest effects in autocracies, where who appear to substantially influence both economic growth and the evolution of political institutions. I shall indicate to explain why substantial roles for individual leaders and national institutional change, which can further influence the growth environment. In the past, examinations of the fundamental causes of growth debate between institutions, culture and geography, which typically operate without reference to the actions of particular personalities. However, economists may imagine leaders indirectly as policymakers, leaders, themselves educational level are rarely the subject of focus.

The constraints imposed on leaders from electoral pressures, opposition parties, independent legislatures and judiciaries all vary across countries. To the extent that the authority embedded in formal institutional rules and the authority embedded in individuals act as substitutes, the increasing visibility of institutional variation in explaining paths may indirectly motivate leaders' behaviors. Theories of economic growth that emphasize public products, e.g. education, health, public entertainment facilities, such as parks, swimming pools etc. Also, national policies include international trade, monetary policy and fiscal policy etc. or all suggest possibly important roles for a national leader.

However, identifying a causative effect of leaders' educational level on economic growth is challenging. Even, if it has relationship between particular leaders' educational level and particular economic growth in particular economic environment. However, it may be that growth changes drive leadership changes, without a causative effect of leaders' educational level. Assumption that a leader quality is independently, it seems the leader has no influence on economic growth. An important additional assumption is that the leader effects are strongest in autocratic settings, especially in the absence of political parties or legislatures to support the leader's any personal view points to achieve any regulations to influence economic growth effectively. These results point to an important effect between institutions and leader individuals in understanding economic growth paths. However, it seems institutions can influence the impact of national leaders behaviors and that national leaders can also influence the path of institutions. If leaders can influence economic growth, then may further these questions are raised: Do leaders act to obstruct economic growth or do they actively promote it? In this view, leaders can be actively good for economic growth, e.g. by investing in public products, choosing pro-growth trade policies, or overcoming national scale coordination problems. However, related questions of how leaders influence growth are related to the role of national policies in explaining growth. If policies might be well matter, even if leaders do not, if national policies care the expression of broader social forces. So, it seems national policies can also influence economic growth, instead of the leader's personal quality or whose educational level. So, it can get this question and conclusion. When asking how do we make poor countries rich? The unexplained, non-deterministic past of economic growth variation becomes especially relevant and given the results about leadership, more within reach.

Human development outsourcing educational strategy

Promoting honesty in negotiation can influence social economy growth in global. In a competitive and moral imperfect world, business people are often facing with serious ethical challenges. Usually, many businessmen feel justified in engaging in less than ideal conduct to protect their own interests. However, our commonplace that work to promote credibility, trust and honesty of behaviours can influence our social economy growth in long term. For example, deception in negotiation behaviour is immoral, due to success in business typically requires successful negotiations. Given the high value placed on honesty, the incentives for deception in negotiation create a serious moral tension for business people. Not surprisingly, deception in negotiation is a widely discussed problem in business ethics. How many negotiators their views are essentially, who is regarded as a superior moral philosopher, would find them objectionable? For example, philosophical debates about the loss of civilian life in war would be better served by putting resources and intellectual energy into developing political, economic diplomatic and military strategies that resources and intellectual energy how to be chosen to use in military strategies aspect or political aspect or economic diplomatic aspect. The country's leader whose educational knowledge will influence the whole country's social economy development in long term. However, individual and social stability are difficult to maintain in a social setting in which there is serious conflict between ethics and personal welfares. Because irrational honesty behaviour is usually caused between the personal welfare and ethics choice.

Whether behavioral economy can be applied to inform and develop human development or /and outsourcing strategy policy effectively. Such policies stress that changing the way choices are presented or changing the environment in which decisions are made, can substantially alter behavior. Ideas from behavioral economics have helped to develop the traditional economic choice framework, in which people are assumed to make choices that are rational, self interested and consistent. Some of the most important behavioral insights for tax and benefit policy include: Faced with complicated decisions, people may make choices, which are often approximately optimal, in that who maximize welfare, but might in some cases lead to poor choices.

There is evidence that how choices are presented affects outcomes. The environment in which decisions are made would provide cues to make particular choices or made could provide cues to make particular choices, or some aspects of the choice problem may be more or less influence to consumers. When any policy relates to income and spending, or it is label money for another can affect what people choose to do with it. Individuals appear to care not just about their own outcomes, but also about those of others. This might be because people derive value from fairness and cooperation. These motivations could give intrinsic incentive to make particular choices. It is possible that providing extrinsic incentives, such as taxes, fines or rewards could be crowded our desirable behavior.

Consumers may have to exercise costly self control to make certain choices, such as eating health foods or giving up smoking. Commitment devices to help overcome self control problems are therefore values, for example, raising the cost of tempting choices, increasing cigarette taxes, say: when making choices with uncertain outcomes, people will do a number of behavioral features. Such as, attaching subjective decision weights to each outcome and these may differ from objective measures of probability.

Usually, outcomes are measured against a reference point, relative to the reference point are felt more strongly than equivalent gains. When welfare increases and ever bigger gains falls, as the welfare cost is from ever bigger losses, then people will appear to be risk seekers when welfare cost comes to cause social loss. How people value the future changes with the passage of time. Usually people hope to earn immediate rewards in present than distant rewards in the future. This means that people make plans who find it hard to achieve. People may also make choices under the assumption that their preferences won't change in the future. So, for policymakers those biases have important implications for why behavior change interventions may be necessary.

Behavioral insights provide new reasons to intervene, issues of self control, for example, making failure, where outcomes are come from the perspective of either individuals or society or both usually. As a common failure is the case of externalities, when individual choices generate costs or benefits for others. Since, these are not taken into account in private decision making, which are come from a social perspective, there is too much or too little of the activity. In this case, taxes or subsidies can help private and social incentives. So, behavioral economical concept can be suggested these important insights for externalities, such as private decisions are closer to the social optimum, reducing the need for correcting taxes or subsidies. It seems that taxes or subsidies will affect to change people's behaviors if social preferences are important. Externalities can arise not just because of how someone affects the well being of others, but also through how decisions made today affect the individual in the future. This is known as an internality. Taxes or subsidies policies both can influence people's present behaviors to be changed and future behaviors will be influenced to be changed from whose present behaviors in societies. Thus, policymakers can not neglect human development or/and outsoucing strategy policy of method to attempt to solve any social challenge nowadays.

Finally, why behavioral economy can assist human development or/and outsourcing policy development. Behavioral economy is a science, includes psychology, economics, finance and sociology to understand human behavior and decision making. Behavioral economics recognizes that constraints in time and mental resources prevent us from optimally evaluating every decision. To deal with our limitations, so we rely on mental decision to judge our face of uncertainty, but we can be leaded to predictably irrational behaviors from behavioral economical concept.

As government agencies enact laws and regulations that are focused in the society. They often rely on restrictions, incentives or public information campaigns in order to change citizen behavior. When well intentioned, those traditional approaches can be accepted. For example, regulations that can be supported to financial advisers disclose conflicts of interest have led to achieve any final results. Disclosures can increase pressures on advisees to comply with the advice provided and in some cases increase greater perceptions of trust rather than the evaluation of biased advice. Similarly, tax incentives can increase retirement savings rates which have had limited impact. Researchers studying the impact of concluded that such policies are an expensive way of encouraging new savings.

On the one hand, governments ought engage their citizens to do any action, whose action is influenced by behavioral economics to discover how behavioral economics can be provided powerful insights into human motivation and behavior. As different countries' government experiments are more from academic laboratories to the real world. So, it is a kind of method to be applied to assist any countries' governments how to use effective policy to improve people's lives. For example, designing what is the best reasonable taxes, subsidies, incentives or educational campaigns level at the rate, donations and retirement savings rates as well as healthy food product label consumption of selection etc. strategic policies which are related how to apply behavioral economy to analyze or experiment to gain the better choice among of them.

On the another hand, Economic agents ought attempt to spend time to gather data to choose to do the best decision, but not perfectly national ones. Also economic research should be used reasonable assumptions about agents' cognitive actives. So, economic models should take predictions that are consistent with micro-level data on decisions, including experimental evidence. Moreover, economists ought spend much time to learn from psychologists.

Behavioral economists now routinely combine experimental data, field data and theory to construct their arguments. As behavioral economic continues to gain acceptance, behavioral economists will increasingly find themselves participating in policy discussions. As policy has the ability to do good or to create great mislead, depending on who, leader is in charge of making the rules. Indeed in some cases the findings of behavioral economists suggest that active policies may be quite harmful. Successful policy analysis should be concerned the motives of private actors, e.g. consumers and firms and the public or governmental actors need to design formulate and enforce policy with cooperation to regulators, bureaucrats, politicians. So, human development and/or outsourcing strategy policy analysis must also be carefully concerned the institutional environment in which these private and public actors interact, e.g. , market, elections and bureaucracies. However, any bad decision making is caused from bounded rationality, slow learning, framing and lack of self control with those effects in mind, one might conclude that government can easily improve consumers' welfare by paternalistically helping consumers make better decisions. Such paternalistic policies can improve consumer welfare by enhancing an individual's maximizing whose own welfare. So, this stands in contrast to most public policies, which address externalities or public products problems that arise because of interactions among economic agents.

To conclude, psychology and behavioral economy and public policy which have close relationship to influence human development and/or outsourcing strategy achievement. As if the national leader had health psychology, then who will have more possible to achieve good behavior to perform to decide how to achieve any the best public policies to raise growth to make welfare to whose citizens. So any policymakers ought need to concern how to listen to behavioral scientists to let them to give any recommendation how to improve or review or revise whose psychological challenges to let them have more effort to decide how to choose to do the right decision effectively. Because the relationship between psychology and behavioral science has more generally to influence public policy which is particularly painful and frustrating of the success for any similar policy recommendations. Hence, economics and psychology indeed can provide human development and/or outsourcing strategy policymakers with vital tools to develop the best policy to solve any social challenges.

Consequently, it seems the leader's psychology will influence whose behavioral performance to be decided to choose to do the more correct policy to influence economic development more easily. It also means that one leader's psychology is an important factor to influence any social economic development directly for long term. So who can not neglect to concern whether whose psychological mind is right or wrong to already to make any decisions to plan any policies before whose any polices are implemented. Because the leader's psychology will influence whose behavior is more correct to decide to decide how to do any policies effectively.

Researching the relationship between education and productivity how to influence economic growth in developing Asia countries nowadays, this topic is concerned how to use labor economy method to analyze how to influence education to cause what the macro and micro economic effects are in the developing Asia countries. I shall indicate some developing countries in Asia, e.g. Philippines, Korea, China etc. countries. What the link between education and productivity is? What does the model that characterize key featured of growth processes of Asia countries are? For this topic, I shall suppose human capital is come from such as primary and secondary and tertiary education factor which has a major close relationship to cause the developing Asia countries' economic growth nowadays. My objectives of this research are to explore the relationship between graduates and economic growth, assess what should be the key variable (or variables) of interest and quantify the relationship to developing Asia of some countries.

Human capital has ability and efficiency of labor to transform raw materials and capital into products and services to affect economic growth. The accumulation of human capital improves labor productivity and increases the returns to capital. However, a well educated background is essential to raise technology to develop economic growth in Asia developing countries especially.

In macro and micro economic view, the well educated labor (human capital) is often as one of the critical factors to influence rapid economic growth to the Asia developing countries' any regions or cities. Because any of these Asia developing countries, such as China, Korea, Philippines etc. countries which need have well educated and knowledgeable labors to raise any employers' productivities and income growth. So productivity and education factor which ought have close relationship to cause the good or bad economic growth in these any one of Asia developing countries. For example, China was an major industrial and farming country between 1960 year and 2000 year. However, after 2000 year, it began to achieve any commercial investment to raise GDP income and to raise more service provision nature of employment chance to domestic labors. e.g. financial investment, shares trading, hotels and tourism and airlines and restaurants and cinemas etc. service nature businesses commercial investment. Moreover, the foreign investors were also attracted to set up factories to manufacture their products in China's country any area locations. It was possible that this foreign investors felt China's workers' wages were more cheaper than themselves domestic worker wages. For example, USA has the minimum wage legislation to protect it's domestic individual worker wage level. Otherwise, China's individual worker wage level is compared to be paid more lower level to compare to USA's minimual legislative individual worker wage level nowadays. It seems China, Korea, Philippines etc. Asia developing countries need have well educated labors to help them to develop economic growth. Because the developed countries' foreign well educated labors, e.g. USA, UK etc. who feel whose countries can give the best salary compensation level and benefits to let them to support to work and to live in whose countries. So the developed countries' well educated labors won't choose to go to China to work very easily. It seems those developing Asia countries which governments need to invest in education sector to increase many knowledgeable human labors capital to assist them to raise whose technological productivity or service productivity or factory productivity to achieve economic growth for long term. If any one of these Asia developing Asia countries still want to keep the competitive position in global environment in the future. So, these Asia developing countries must need good education to train any aspects of high knowledgeable labors to supply to themselves society to work in essential.

Ha, Kim and Lee (2009) provided evidence to indicate that "using panel data covering from 1989 year to 2000 year in Japan, Korea and Taipei, China as the distance to the technology frontier narrows basis research and development (R&D) investment, i.e. highly skilled labor which showed the higher growth effect than development R&D investment , i.e. less skilled labor. They also provided evidence that the quality of tertiary education has a significantly positive effect on the productivity of R&D.

Nowadays, education is commonly regarded as the most direct influence to people out of poverty owing to the tendency for employment opportunities especially for higher skilled workers to be created in Asia developing countries. In fact, raising productivity is depended on the quantity and quality of human resource, which itself largely depends on investment in education theoretical linkages between education and growth. Generally, growth theory suggests that economic growth depends on the accumulation of economic, including human assets and the return on these assets, which depend on technological progress, the efficiency which assets are being used. So, growth theory which emphasizes on the centrality of human capital for innovation and technological progress. However, the theory indicates of policy ineffectiveness which characterizes the neo-classical growrh theory by giving importance to the production of new technologies and human capital development. So focusing on factors within the model rather than relying on external factors. It seems the economists of supporting growth believe that improvements in productivity are linked to a faster pace of innovation and extra investment in human capital. Also these economists of supporting growth theory emphasize on the need for governments and private sector educational institutions and job markets for tertiary students' demand and to innovate knowledgeable of social economy to actively provide incentives for individual student to become inventive in any countries. They also identify the central role of knowledge as determinant of economic growth. Hence, growth theory can predict positive externalities and spillover effects from development of a high valued-added knowledge economy to the development and maintenance of a competitive advantage across the global.

Why do I research the relationship between education and productivity can influence the economic growth to Asia developing countries? Although, human capital includes education, health and aspects of social capital. The main focus of the present study is on education. The analysis stresses the distination between the quantity of education measured by years of attainment at various levels and the quality measured by scores on internationally comparable examinations, e.g. China education and Korea education comparision. In fact, the global long term economic growth was the central macroeconomic problem and it was fortunately accompanied in the late 1980 year by importance advances in the theory of economic growth. This period featured the development of global growth models, in which the long term rate of growth was determined within the model.

A key feature of these models is a theory of technological progress, viewed as a process whereby purposeful research and application lead over time to new and better products and methods of production by developed economic globalization. The recent growth models are useful for understanding why advanced economies and the world is as whole, can continue to grow in the long run despite the workings of diminishing returns in the accumulation of physical and human capital. These countries include, e.g. America, England which are observed to be rich and high tend also to be those that have high long run target levels of per high capita output in a setting that includes human capital and technological change. So education is also essential to raise labour knowledge and technological level to assist developed countries, e.g. USA, UK , to raise productivity to achieve economic growth. So, the developed or developing countries' both government policies and education institutions need to concern their national population to arrange the different primary, secondary and tertiary educational policy to educate to develop whose students to develop different professional and knowledgeable and skillful abilities to already develop their careers in different nature of jobs to enter their societies to work nowadays. However, if we were the identify how education contributes to cause economic growth in any Asia developing countries. We need to compare states that have a similar distance to the frontier and yet choose difference pattern of investment in education. For example, building a new school for a research university, the process is when a vacancy arises on an committee that controls expenditure. Because governments and universities need to concern what the labour market demand, so the research university can decide prefer to choose what kinds of subjects to be taught to its potential students, e.g. medical or architect or law or engineering or business or social science, computer science etc. subjects among of them subjects, which subjects will be chosen to be taught to its potential students preferably. So, the job demand market research is very important because it can help the research university to choose what the preferable subjects will be demanded to supply to the labour market increasing in any one of Asia developing countries within future three or five years.

Theories of economic growth have emphasised the role of human capital which may affect economic growth. Human capital is as an extra input in the aggregate production function, where the output of the means economy is a direct function of factor inputs: physical capital, labor and human capital. However, technologies can raise innovate capacity of economy through developing new ideas. So, education was seemed that it could be raised graduated students' abilities to raise productivity to any one of Asia developing countries by high technological skill.

How outsourcing education strategy influences
economy development to Asia countries

Any countries have two different channels through which human capital can affect long run economic growth by education provision. The first channel is when human capital is a direct input in the production function and the second channel is when the human capital affects the technology parameter. The result establishes a long run relationship between education and economic growth. A well educated labour force appears to significantly influence economic growth both as a factor in the production function and through total factor productivity. With its large resources of human and natural resources, the potential to build a prosperous economy to reduce poverty significantly and to provide the health, education services that its population needs. As the Asia developing countries, e.g. China or Korea, which are poor countries past years, which need foreign investors' different businesses development in their countries. So, themselves education is commonly regarded as the most direct avenue to rescue a substantial number of people out of poverty since there is likely to be more employment opportunities and higher wages for skilled workers. Furthermore, education can enable children's attitudes and assists them to grow up with social values that are more benefitical to their nations and themselves.

The theoretical basis of education on economic growth is rooted in the endogenous growth theory. Endogenous growth economists believe that improvements in productivity can be linked to a faster pace of innovation and extra investment in human capital. Engogenous growth theorists argue the need for government and private sector institutions and markets which need to innovate and provide incentives for individuals to be inventive. There is also a central role for knowledge as a determinant of economic growth theory can predict positive externalities and spill over effects from development of a high valued-added knowledge economy which is able to develop and maintain a competitive advantage in growth industries in the global economy.

Nowadays, education at levels countries to economic growth through imparting general attitudes and discipline and special skills necessary for a variety of work places. It contirbutes to economic growth by improving health, reducing fertility and possibly by contributing to political stability to different developing or developed both countries. The major importance of the educational system to any labor market would depend majority in ability to produce a literate, disciplines, flexible labor force via high quality education. Consequently, with economic development new technology is applied to production with results in an increase in the demand for workers and better education. In the developing countries, e.g. China, Korea, rich individuals allocate labor time not only for their own production and knowledge accumulation, but also train the poor individuals. In the past, some economists estimated a model of economic growth and human capital accumulation based on a sample of developing countries, e.g. China, Korea etc. are not a different stage of development. Their result revealed that the increase in the primary and secondary countries to an increase in productivity. They indicate that human capital acccumulation rates are affected by demographic variables. For example, they established that an increase in life expectancy at birth brings about an increase in secondary and tertiary education when a decrease in the dependence rate negatively affects secondary education. Finally, they added that geographic variables have a considerable importance in the human capital accumulation process. Nevertheless, studies differed on the impact of human capital on productivity.

The economists also indicate that human capital accumulation rates are affected by demographic variables as well as the increase in the primary and secondary level of education contibutes to an increase in productivity. For example, they established that a increase in life expectancy at birth brings about an increase in secondary and tertiary education when a decrease in the dependence rate negatively affects secondary education. However, who also believe the overall results of secondary and higher education can have a significant positive impact on growth, when primary education had not contributed to economic growth.

The GDP per unit of labor input should be related to the share of labor of a particular type (graduates or workers at different qualification levels) weighted by the average human capital of the type of worker (captured by the relative wages of different types of labor input). It seems measure of the relationship between education and productivity and economic growth can be quantified clearing to developing Asia any countries.

In past, the EUKLEMS project indicated key findings of 15 developed countries for one economic report: GDP per employment hour increased from 1992 year to 2005 year, the highest annual average percentage change was in Finland (2.7%), Japan (2.5%) and the UK (2.4%). These countries had the lowest level of GDP per employment hour in 1982 year, when the period considered the Netherlands and the USA had the highest GDP employment hour. Also it indicated the share of employment with tertiary education also increased from 1982 year to 2005 year in all countries. The highest annual average percentage change was in Australia (5%) followed by the UK (4.9%). Both of these countries had relatively low shares of employment with tertiary education in 1982 year at 6%, compared with 22.1% in the USA and 18.7% in Finland. The large increased closed the gap, but the USA and Finland still had higher employment shares with tertiary education than Australia and the UK in 2005 year. The economic report also indicatd that a 1% increase in the share of the workforce with a university degree raises the level of long run productivity by 0.2%-0.5%. So, it implied the education and productivity has close relationship to developed countries also. However, the economic benefits, both to the individual and to the wider economy of a university degree with clearly depend on the quality and skills to developing and developed countries both.

So, improvement in educational outcomes have been widely recognised as essential in enhancing growth in both developed and developing countries. In fact, education is acquire by individuals provide social returns at the macroeconomic level and addition indirect benefits to economic growth.

Firstly, I suppose it has relationship between human capital and education has close relationship to cause economic growth to any developed or developing countries both nowadays. Because if human capital and education factor has close relationship to influence any country's economic growth, then it is possible to cause productivity and economic growth has close relationship. However, some economists indicate the evidence on the relationship between human capital and economic growth and who conclude that there is strong evidence that human capital increases productivity. Suggesting that education really is productivity-enhancing, rather than education is used by individuals to signal their ability to potential employers.

The primary measures are used to capture the average level of human capital per worker include:

I. The average number of years of schooling of the workforce or population, which assumes a linear relationship with human capital.

II. The share of the workforce population with specific educational qualifications.

III. School enrolment rates, specially as a starting value. This flow into education is often used as stock of qualifications and is available for developed Asia countries, e.g. Hong Kong, Japan and developing Asia countries, e.g. China, Korea both.

However, developing Asia countries have potential problems arising from measurement errors in education, as the average schooling levels are derived from enrolment flows. They adopt more reliable country level education micro data and find a positive result or response between the growth rate of education and economic growth. Human capital flows are most commonly provided by school enrolment rates, have been widely used in studies of the relationship between human captial and growth. This is largely due to the availability of long time series of data for a large developing or developed both Asia or foreign countries rather than because it is viewed as proferable to the human captial stock of education measures. So, based on the motivation that school enrolment rates conflate human capital stock and accumulation effects and lead to misinterpretations of the role of labor force growth. It seems education may be one of method to raise human capital and productivity growth to cause any developed or developing Asia or foreign countries' economic growth for long term nowadays.

Recently, the research indicates the impact of education quality is mixed. Moreover, recent studies actually suggest that education quantity is unrelated to economic growth at least in developed countries. On the other hand, a growing literature focuses on the growth impact of education quality, measures by international test scores. It finds a strong effect of education quality on economic growth when confirming that education quantity is irrelevant apart from via its impact on quality. So, I suggest the developing Asia countries' governments, e.g. China, Korea should continue their market based reforms in education. For example, by streamlining the requirements and process to establish new free schools. The goals should be to expand parental choice as widely as possible. Because education might be way to personal fulfilment, but it can also be an instrument for a healthy economy. So, reforming the education system could be a key part of any long term growth strategy to any Asia developing countries. For example, whose governments can increase spending significantly, when gradually raising the compulsory education age from 16 to 18 age following the education and skills act. Also expanding the average number of years spent in education be sufficient to improve growth. Also, any one of Asia developing countries can raise education quality more important that how much education one receives , i.e. education quantity? And how education policy can secure the highest economic dividend in as reduce efficient manner as possible. The policy implication is clear the Asia developing countries' governments should encourage an increase in the enrolment shares of independently operated schools, for example by streamlining the requirements and process to establish new free schools. A voucher system with which pupils can attend the school of their choice, either public or independent would be preferable. Such a system would sharpen competitive incentives in the education system significantly. Thus increasing the potential for choice to produce an economic dividend.

Why is education presumed to affect economic growth in any one of Asia developing countries? The main reason given is that it should improve the overall skill level, or human capital of the labor force. How human capital may be related to economic growth. Usually, capital growth is only determined by capital accumulation and technological changes. In the growth model, only technological innovation can explain long term growth because capital accumulation effects suffer from diminishing and returns. Technological change is thus the sole determinant of growth once an economy's new equilibrium/steady state (zero growth states is reached. At the same time, the sources of technological change, such as human captial are assumed to be not included as an explanatory variable in the model. In other words, the model treats education as a residual rather than as integral part of the process of change in explaining an economy's per-capita growth rate. Thus, some economists do not believe education is a conceptual tool to assist economic growth. However, some economists believe technological change and education can assist economic growth when these two factors are same to exist. Thus, education can impact growth not only by affecting innovation directly. But also by aiding the adoption of existing technology.

The augmented assumed that the effect of education eventually growth models allow education at any given level to continue to impact growth through its effect on technological change and diffusion in the economy. In other meaning, education can be provide to students to raise high technological human capital to assist economic growth. So, education can be treated as a regular factor of production to affect the growth rate in the subsequent period. This has implications for how the education variable should be included in statistical analyses, which has been a subject of debate. Otherwise, most research has focused mostly on education quantity,such as the average number of years of schooling. For example, some older studies used school enrolment rates as a measure of education. Enrolment rates impacts are being used different growth periods average over the period. It also indicates that increasing enrolment rates are positive for economic growth in developing Asia countries, e.g. China , Korea etc. In conclusion, it seems education quantity and quality as well as productivity has also relationship to influence developing Asia countries' economic growth for long term. Moreover, Asia countries choose outsourcing education which can raise students' educational level because which lack more experienced and high educational quality teachers to educate whose students. Thus, overseas teachers teach to Asia countries can give more benefits to Asia students. than Asia domestic teachers

Reference

Abrahamson, E., & Rosenkopf., (1993). Institutional and competitive bandwagons: Using mathematicalmodeling and a tool to explore innovation diffusion.

Academy of management review, 18(3), 487-517.

Hill, C.W.L. & Jones, G.R. 1995. Strategic management, An integrated approach. Boston: Houghtom Mif In.

Dimson, Marsh & Staunton, London Business School (2005) In The Global Investment Returns Year Book, ABN Amro.

Fiscal Policy And Long Term Growth, International Monetary Fund, IMF policy papers, Washington, D.C. Available from April, 2015, http://www.imf.org/external/pp/ppindex.aspx.

Kim, Y. J., and J.W. Lee 2009. Technological Change, Human Capital Structure and Multiple Growth Paths, ADB Economics Working Paper Series No. 149, Economics And Research Dept. Asian Development Bank, Manila.